Hand Reading

Discover your future

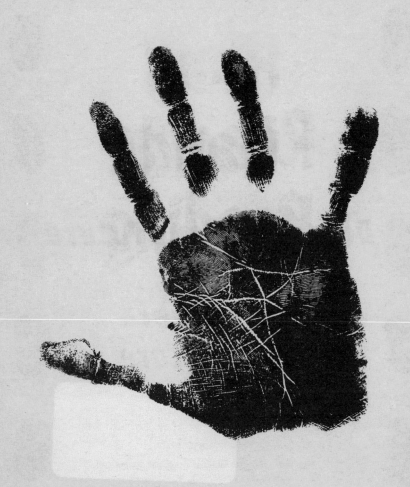

Hand
Reading

Discover your future

LORI REID

Illustrated by Paul Dowling

SCHOLASTIC INC.
New York Toronto London Auckland Sydney
Mexico City New Delhi Hong Kong

ISBN 0-439-07844-X

12 11 10 9 8 7 6 5 4 3 2 1   9/9 0 1 2 3 4/0

Printed in the U.S.A.   40

First Scholastic printing, March 1999

Cover design by Ness Wood
Cover photography: Jon Stone
Designed by The Design Group, 74b High Street, Honiton, Devon EX14 8PD.

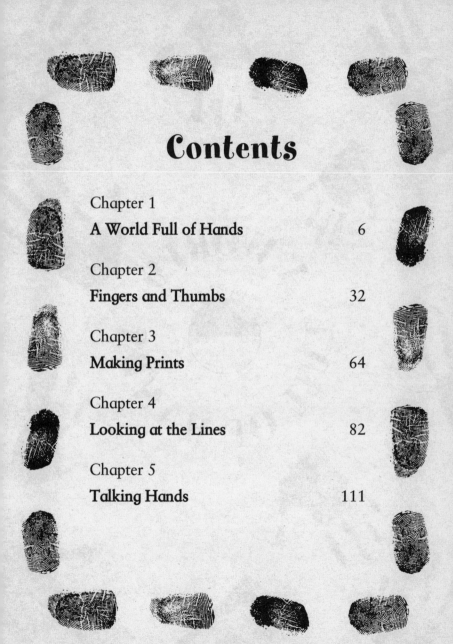

Contents

A WORLD FULL OF HANDS

CHAPTER 1

Do you find waiting at the bus stop boring?

Do you get impatient if you're kept waiting at the check-out in the supermarket? Do you find standing around in assembly excruciatingly dull? If so, the solution is in your own hands - literally! Well, in your own hands and in those of the people around you.

You see, hands are really revealing, so it's not surprising that they have fascinated people for centuries. Hands come in all sorts of different sizes, in a variety of shapes, and in an assortment of colors. Some have thin pointed fingers, some have short stubby thumbs. Some have almond-shaped nails, others have milky-white moons. Some palms are thick and square, some are long and lean. Some hands are so lined you'd think a spider had spun its web into them, while others are so clear you'd be hard pressed to find more than three main lines crossing the palms.

It's these differences that make hands so fascinating because, as you'll soon find out, our hands are a reflection of our personalities. The palm contains more nerve endings than anywhere else on the body, so you could say that your palm is like a computer print-out of what is going on in your brain. In fact, our hands are like identikit pictures of our identities and once you know what the different shapes and patterns mean, you will be able to tell what a person is like - even a complete stranger.

You'll be able to say with confidence whether a person is patient or short-tempered, practical or artistic. By a mere glance at people's hands, you will know who is sporty, who is intelligent, who likes collecting things, who's a good cook, who's musical, who's dreamy or lazy, or even, who can't resist telling the odd fib.

So you see... once you know about hand reading, just a glimpse of someone's hands will give you clues about that person's character. The more you know about the meaning of the...

SHAPES LINES LUMPS AND BUMPS

the more you will be able to discover about what other people are like. In fact, you'll soon be able to read a person as if you were reading a book.

And that's why, when you know a bit about hand reading, waiting for a bus need never be boring again!

Let's Get Down to Business

The very first thing to notice about a person's hand is its shape. You'd be surprised how much information you can pick up just by spotting what type of hand a person possesses.

When you first start to observe hands, you'll think that each one you see is different - which is absolutely true! Every hand is indeed unique.

Of course, every person in the world is unique, too, yet we can classify people into different categories according to their similarities. For example, we can group people into men and women, short people and tall people, young and old. We can sort them by their nationalities - Chinese or Indian or Australian or whatever. Or by the jobs they do - bus drivers, nurses, engineers, and so on.

In exactly the same way, all hands can be grouped into four different types. These four types are known as Earth hands, Air hands, Fire hands and Water hands. It can be a little tricky at first to work out which group a hand belongs to, but the more hands you examine, the better you'll become at telling them apart.

THE FOUR H

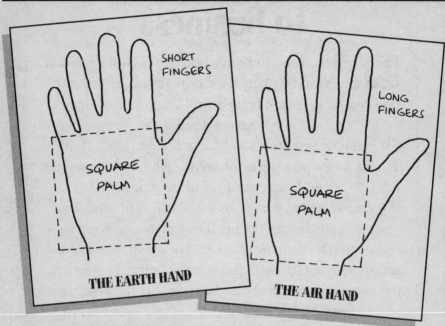

SHORT FINGERS

SQUARE PALM

THE EARTH HAND

LONG FINGERS

SQUARE PALM

THE AIR HAND

Basically, you just need to remember two rules:
1. **THE PALM IS EITHER SQUARE OR OBLONG**
2. **THE FINGERS ARE EITHER SHORT OR LONG**
By combining these two rules, you get the four shapes (see diagrams).

Don't expect every hand to fit into these shapes perfectly. Some, you'll find, have rounded outside edges, or sharp angles beneath the thumb, or are much wider at the top of the palm than at the wrist. All you can do is get each hand as close to the categories as you can. If in doubt, go back to

AND GROUPS

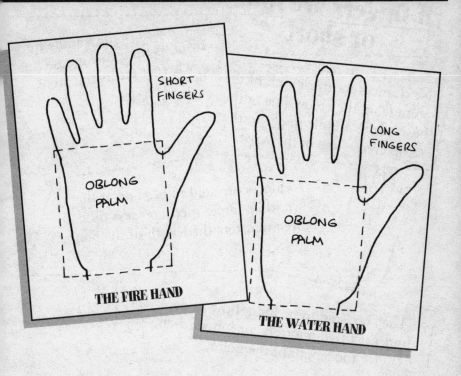

SHORT FINGERS

OBLONG PALM

THE FIRE HAND

LONG FINGERS

OBLONG PALM

THE WATER HAND

the basic rules and ask yourself, 'Is this palm squarish in shape (that is, as wide as it is long), or does it look oblong (that is, longer than it is wide)?' Once you've made that decision, you must then judge whether the fingers are short or long.

This is perhaps the most difficult decision that you have to make in hand reading. However, once you have made it, you can really get cracking and then the fun begins.

How you can tell if fingers are long or short

First, measure the middle finger from its tip to the crease line where it meets the palm.

Next, measure the length of the palm from the crease line at the base of the middle finger to the top crease line at the wrist.

Fingers are said to be short if the middle finger measures less than three-quarters the length of the palm.

They are said to be long if the middle finger is three-quarters, or longer than, the length of the palm.

You can take these measurements directly from the person's hand, but it's often easier to work from a hand print. You'll find instructions and a list of the materials you will need for taking hand prints on pages 76-77.

LEFT or RIGHT

One of the first questions people ask when they begin to read their hands is, 'Which hand should I look at, my right or my left hand?'

The simple answer is that you should look at both. However, to begin with, just concentrate on your dominant hand. That is, the one you use most. So, if you're left-handed study the left one, and if you're right-handed study the right one.

The whole area of right- and left-handedness is a fascinating business and you can find out more about it on pages 79-81.

The Earth Hand

How to spot the Earth hand
- squarish palm
- short fingers
- fingertips are often blunt or square
- the palm usually contains few lines but these are strong and clearly marked

The character that goes with the Earth hand

People who possess Earth-shaped hands are hard-working and practical. They love making things and are especially gifted with their hands. Born with masses of common sense, they think logically and are never afraid to speak their minds. They are honest and truthful and you always know where you stand with them.

As friends, they're solid and reliable and if you ever need their help, they will stop whatever they're doing and be there for you in a flash. However, don't expect them to take silly risks or chances - that's not in their character and they're very uncomfortable if they break the rules.

Earth-handed people are rarely moody or easily upset because they're emotionally steady and level-headed, so it takes a lot to make them cry. If they do, you can be sure that something has affected them very, very deeply.

As well as being brilliant at handicrafts, they usually excel at sports and what Earth-handed people like best is being out in the fresh air and in the great outdoors. They start fidgeting if they're cooped up inside for too long, so it's important for them to go out and play football, go for a ride on their bikes or take the dog for a walk. Most of the people belonging to this category are close to nature. Many have either green fingers or a special rapport with animals.

People with Earth-type hands like
- working with their hands
- playing sports
- owning pets
- making models
- gardening
- sticking to a routine
- cooking

They should be encouraged to
- have a good night's sleep - every night
- take plenty of exercise in the fresh air
- eat a healthy diet

Earth-handed people should avoid
- stress
- sitting around watching too much television
- thinking that a situation is hopeless

The Air Hand

How to spot the Air hand
- squarish palm
- long fingers
- fingertips are often rounded
- the palm contains several lines which are clear and well defined

The character that goes with the Air hand

People with this type of hand are flexible and adaptable and love anything to do with communications. They have lively, intelligent minds, take a keen interest in everything and everyone around them and can talk the hind legs off a donkey! At school, those who excel at reading, writing, and languages are more often than not people who possess this type of hand.

In particular, these people are noted for being quick learners. All an Air-handed person has to do is watch something being done once and he or she will pick it up in the twinkling of an eye. There is one problem with this sort of quick mentality, however, and that is they get bored very quickly, so people belonging to this group need lots of hobbies to keep their interest alive.

Gadgets of all kinds fascinate these inventive folk and it doesn't take long for them to become computer whiz kids. If they could, they would probably spend the whole evening on the telephone, chatting away to the many friends and acquaintances they tend to gather around them throughout their lives.

People with Air-type hands like
- being witty
- reading
- working on the computer
- talking, talking, talking
- learning something new
- hi-tech equipment
- lots of variety

They should be encouraged to
- finish what they start
- learn a subject in depth instead of just skimming the surface
- take their talents seriously

Air-handed people should avoid
- scattering their energies
- trying to be in two places at once
- talking so much that they fail to hear what others are trying to tell them

The Fire Hand

How to spot the Fire hand
- oblong palm
- short fingers
- fingertips are often wide
- the palm contains a good number of strong lines

The character that goes with the Fire hand

Physically active and dynamic, Fire-handed people are always on the go. They have energy to burn and need adventure and excitement to spice up their lives. That's why so many of them become brilliant sportsmen and women, fearlessly plunging headlong from the highest diving board, climbing the sheerest cliff face, or braving the rollers on a surf board.

In fact, these people are never far from the centre of the action - or for that matter, from the spotlight. They're actors at heart with a love for drama in life. If there's an end-of-year production, you can be sure these people will be the first to put their names down for the starring role. Many go on to work in show business or in the entertainment world when they leave school.

If you're feeling low, these are the people you need around you. With their fun-loving, happy-go-lucky characters, they know just what to do to cheer you up. Indeed, Fire-handed people are the life and soul of the party, and are blessed with the gift of spreading enthusiasm and inspiration wherever they go.

Members of this group make natural leaders, not only because they are brave and like to be at the front of the action, but also because they understand people and have the ability to inspire and motivate them. Wherever the Fire hand goes, it seems, others tend to follow.

People with Fire-type hands like
- excitement and adventure
- entertaining people and making them laugh
- being on the go
- performing and showing off
- being in charge
- organizing
- pioneering or breaking records

They should be encouraged to
- calm their minds and bodies (with music, yoga or a soothing hobby)
- channel their energies into regular exercise or sports
- learn how to pace themselves

Fire-handed people should avoid
- rushing, as this often leads to accidents
- leaving things until the last minute
- eating too much rich or spicy food, or taking stimulants of any kind

The Water Hand

How to spot the Water hand
- oblong palm
- long fingers
- fingertips are often rounded or pointed
- the palm is covered in a jumble of fine lines like cobwebs

The character that goes with the Water hand

Water-handed people excel in the arts. Painting, pottery, sculpture, dressmaking, crafts, and design are all favorite subjects. With their exceptional patience and their terrific eye for detail, they can spend hours tracing tiny patterns or coloring in intricate or elaborate pictures.

Music is a special love of theirs and many will play in an orchestra. But so too is literature and, more especially, poetry. For these people are poets and thinkers and dreamers, often living with their heads in the clouds - which gets them into trouble for day-dreaming and not paying enough attention in class.

People with Water-shaped hands are perhaps the most sensitive and gentle of the four types. Often, they are shy and quiet and can be easily upset by rough behavior or noisy outbursts. They suffer a lot if others are unkind to them or call them names. In fact, they really find it hard to deal with aggression of any sort. They will retreat inside themselves at the first sign of trouble, and it's this that gives them a reputation for sulking and moodiness.

These people are emotionally tender and they let their hearts rule their minds. However, it's this very closeness to their feelings that makes them caring and compassionate and able to understand when other people are troubled or in pain.

People with Water-type hands like

- a world filled with beauty and kindness
- to care for people or animals in distress
- dancing, singing and playing music
- drawing and designing
- reading or writing poetry
- beautiful clothes
- a peaceful environment

They should be encouraged to

- build up their confidence
- believe in their talents
- think logically

Water-handed people should avoid

- competitive situations
- getting carried away by their imagination
- becoming moody, melancholic, or depressed

GETTING ON

The four different groups of hands give you a basic idea of the sort of character and personality that belongs to each type. You can use this information to find out how people with different hand shapes get on together. Obviously, people in the same category will understand each other well because they think and behave in the same sort of way.

For example, Air-handed people will all enjoy gossiping and talking to each other about computer programs or mobile phones until the cows come home. Earth-handed people might prefer to go for a long walk together in the country, perhaps have a picnic and look at the wild flowers and woodland creatures. Fire-handed people are quite different. When they get together they would probably prefer

TOGETHER

to thrash each other at tennis, have a cycle race, or explore a new part of town. In contrast, Water-handed people might sit in someone's bedroom and have a marvelous afternoon listening to CDs, flicking through magazines, and discussing the latest fashion trends.

But what happens when the hand shapes mix? Have a look at your own hand shape and compare it with your best friend's hand, or to those of other people around you. Perhaps those you get on with best are the people whose hands are compatible with your own. And perhaps those people you don't like are the ones whose hands are "opposite" to yours.

The Earth Hand

Earth + Earth	Earth + Air	Earth + Fire	Earth + Water
These two get on well together and take life at a similar pace	The Earth-hander gets frustrated by Air's restlessness	Both have a lot of energy and Earth enjoys Fire's enthusiasm	Definite opposites, one lives on the ground and the other in the clouds

The Air Hand

Air + Air	Air + Earth	Air + Fire	Air + Water
These two are definitely on the same wavelength	The inventive Air-handed person finds Earth far too plodding	With a bit of give and take, these two can become good friends	A good team with a lot to offer each other

The Fire Hand

Fire + Fire	Fire + Earth	Fire + Air	Fire + Water
All-action, all-adventure - this is a dynamic duo	Earth is far too cautious for the adventurous Fire	These two are never short of ideas when they're together	Sometimes hot and sometimes cold, this friendship is a bit on and off

The Water Hand

Water + Water	Water + Earth	Water + Air	Water + Fire
A pair of good, supportive and understanding friends	These two are as different as chalk and cheese	This pair have a lot of admiration for each other	The fire-hander could prove a little too hot for Water to handle

Examining the Lumps and Bumps

Have you ever had a really good look at your own palms? Once you start to examine your hands very closely, you begin to notice things about them that you have never noticed before.

For example, you might see that one or two of the lumps and bumps on your palm stand out more than others. Perhaps you discover that some areas are flat while others rise up like little hills. Maybe the outer edge of your palm is very rounded, or dead straight, or slopes in sharply towards your wrist. Have you ever noticed that before? And if you have, did you stop to think what it might mean?

Hold up your hand so that it's level with your eyes, with your palm facing the ceiling. Now, lightly cup your hand and look across it from your wrist all the way to your fingertips. From this position, you'll get a good view of what look like tiny cushion pads stuffed under the skin of your palm. These are called mounts and you may have as many as nine of them. Don't worry, though, if you can't count as many as that because in most hands some of the mounts tend to merge together. On your hand, for example, you might be able to count only five or even fewer mounts.

Hand readers think of the mounts as little areas of energy and, depending on their position on the palm, they tell us a lot about our interests, our strengths and weaknesses, and how we use our talents. If we divide the hand up into sections, we find that each area represents a different aspect of our lives. One area, for instance, can tell us something about our health and vitality, another about our feelings. Other sections will give us clues about how brave we are or whether or not we are interested in science or the arts, and so on.

If you have a large mount on any one of these sections, it means that whatever that area represents is very important in your life. Perhaps you have lots of that particular energy, or are enormously interested in whatever that area is referring to. You may even be especially gifted in this area. In the same way, if a mount appears to be flat, it could mean that you're just not interested in whatever subject that section of your hand represents.

Once you have discovered which mount on your palm is more developed than the others, you will be able to tell where your best talents lie. Similarly, the areas that are least developed will reveal which areas of your life you need to work on. A word of caution, however - when you are comparing your mounts, do remember that the area at the base of the thumb is nearly always larger than the rest, so it will only make a real difference if it is so huge that it appears to dwarf the rest of the palm.

Take a look at the illustration on page 28 that shows the nine mounts. Decide which of those areas stand out in your own hands, then read on to find out what it means about you.

The Nine Mounts

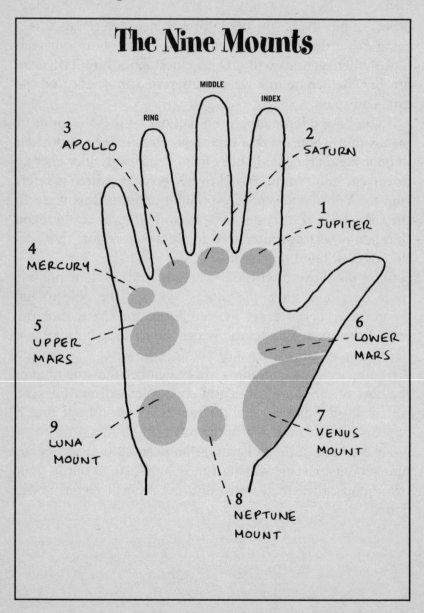

1. The mount of **Jupiter** lies just below the index finger. It tells you about your self-confidence. If the mount here is large, it means you are mature and you can cope well with whatever happens in your life. If it is enormous, it could mean that you are bossy! Alternatively, if the mount looks flat and non-existent, it could be that you lack confidence. If that is so, find out which other areas in your hand are well developed as this will show you where your best talents lie. When you find these, being proud of your abilities should help to boost your morale.

2. The mount of **Saturn** is found beneath the middle finger. It deals with your sense of responsibility and, of all the mounts in the hand, this is the one that should be underdeveloped. The flatter it is, the more

pleased you should be. If it looks built up, check that what you're looking at isn't in fact part of the mounts on either side of it which might be leaning over onto this area. When the area is highly padded it reveals someone who tends to be a bit of a misery and a wet blanket.

3. The mount of **Apollo** lies beneath the ring finger. People with a well-rounded pad here are blessed with a happy and sunny disposition. They also tend to be very creative. If the area is flat, it means the person isn't interested in the arts. If it is huge, it can suggest someone who is snobbish and big-headed.

4. The mount of **Mercury** lies beneath the little finger. It deals with several things. It represents communications, interests in scientific subjects and money. If your

Mercury mount is large, it means you are warm and friendly and love talking to people. If it's the largest mount of the lot, it suggests that you're a terrible chatterbox. Anyone whose mount of Mercury is flat probably lacks a sense of humor.

5. The mount of **Upper Mars** lies directly beneath the mount of Mercury. When this is well padded it reveals people with staying power who don't give up easily. These persons have what is known as moral integrity. They have the courage of their own convictions and will put up with a lot of hassle to be true to their beliefs. People whose mount of Upper Mars is poorly developed find it hard to cope under pressure.

6. The mount of **Lower Mars** is found just above the place where the thumb joins onto the palm. This area represents physical strength and courage. Someone with a good mount here is brave. A lack of development, or even a hollow instead of a mount, suggests someone who is timid. If this area is thickly padded and the mount stands up high, it reveals someone who is aggressive. People with this development should be sure to play a lot of sports so that they can channel their energies and their anger into physical work-outs and not take out their feelings on other people.

7. The mount of **Venus** is beneath the mount of Lower Mars at the base of the thumb. It is usually a large, well-padded area. When this area is well-developed and springy to the touch, it reveals a healthy vitality. Someone

with a mount like this has a lot of energy and can bounce back quickly after an illness. If this area is a bit flabby, it means the person is lazy. If it looks pale and weak, it suggests the person's health could be delicate. This can also reveal someone who is standoffish and selfish. But if this area is huge, the person is very passionate and tends to go over the top in everything he or she does!

8. The mount of **Neptune** is at the base of the palm. It is often underdeveloped, but when it does exist it shows a person who is popular and gets on well with everyone.

9. The mount of **Luna** is found at the base of the palm on the opposite side to the thumb. It represents your imagination, sensitivity, and intuition. When it is overdeveloped and stands up high, it hints at a silly person who can be flighty and moody. If the area is flat, that person lacks imagination. A nicely rounded and springy mount is found in the hand of someone who is a good writer or who loves music and poetry. A very interesting form of this mount is sometimes found. See if you have it in your own hand. It occurs when this mount is developed low down so that it overhangs the wrist and pushes the crease mark down. When it is formed like this, it means that the person has natural rhythm and is a fantastic dancer. Models often have this type of mount and they, of course, carry themselves with wonderful poise which is part and parcel of this natural body rhythm.

CHAPTER 2 — FINGERS AND THUMBS

You have probably drawn around your hands hundreds of times, so you will have a good idea of what your outline looks like. But did you know that even a simple outline of your hand can say a lot about you?

If you want to find out what secrets your outline reveals, you will need a large sheet of paper and a sharp pencil. Just before you place your hand on the paper, shake it for a few seconds to loosen it up, then put it down in whatever position feels natural and comfortable. Don't overstretch your fingers, or bunch them up tightly together, unless of course that is what you would do naturally. What you want is to feel that your hand is resting as comfortably as possible. Starting at the wrist, trace around the palm, thumb and fingers in a flowing line, ending back at the wrist on the opposite side from where you began.

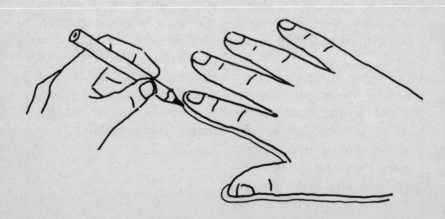

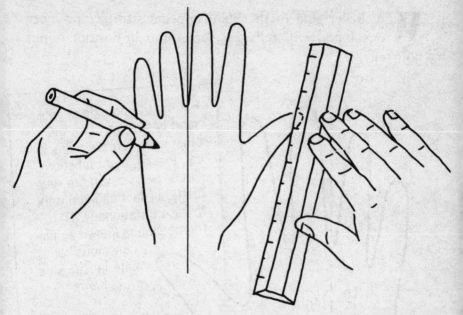

Next, place a ruler down the center of the outline and draw a vertical line starting from the web between the ring and middle finger down to the wrist, to divide the palm in two. Now examine the two halves and note any differences between them.

For instance, you may spot that the fingers and mounts on the thumb side are stronger, meatier, more robust looking than on the other side. Alternatively, perhaps the outer, percussion edge beneath the little finger is very rounded, giving the hand a huge bow-window effect. Or maybe the fleshy bottom mount on one side is massive while the one on the other side is thin, pale, and almost non-existent.

Whichever side of the hand appears stronger or more developed will tell you something important about yourself.

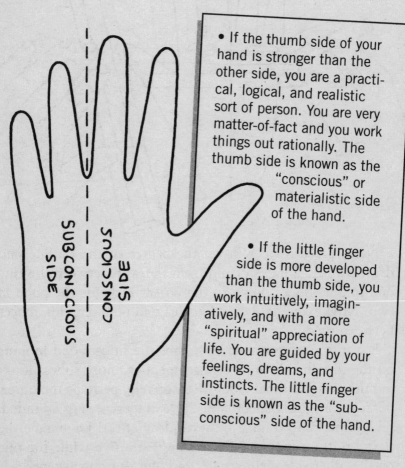

SUBCONSCIOUS SIDE

CONSCIOUS SIDE

- If the thumb side of your hand is stronger than the other side, you are a practical, logical, and realistic sort of person. You are very matter-of-fact and you work things out rationally. The thumb side is known as the "conscious" or materialistic side of the hand.

- If the little finger side is more developed than the thumb side, you work intuitively, imaginatively, and with a more "spiritual" appreciation of life. You are guided by your feelings, dreams, and instincts. The little finger side is known as the "subconscious" side of the hand.

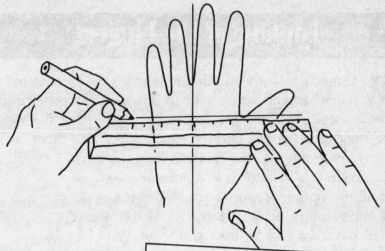

Now place the edge of the ruler just above where the thumb joins onto the palm and draw a horizontal line right across the center of the hand to divide the palm in two. Compare the top and bottom of the palm.

• If your palm is wider across the top edge than it is at the wrist, it shows that you are a thinker, someone who prefers mental rather than physical activity. You probably like reading, writing, mind games, quizzes, and crossword puzzles.

• If the base of your palm is chunkier, broader, or in any way more developed than the top, it means that you are physically strong and have masses of energy. Try to catch sight of the hands of active sports people when they're being interviewed on television and you'll see that this part of their hands is usually hugely developed.

Looking at the Fingers

When you took the outline of your hand, it was important that you put your hand down on the paper in a comfortable position. The reason for this is that the way the fingers are placed, and the spacings between them, will say a lot about you. But you can only get a true picture if the fingers are laid down in a natural position - no unnecessary stretching or undue bunching up, please.

Now take a look at how you placed those fingers. Are they all evenly spaced or would you say that the gaps between some of the fingers are wider than others?

IS THERE...

A WIDE SPACE BETWEEN YOUR INDEX AND MIDDLE FINGERS?

YES - This means you like to think for yourself. You are also ambitious and want to do well in life.

NO - This means you're not happy in the full glare of the spotlight. You're rather shy and prefer others to take the lead.

IS THERE...

A WIDE SPACE BETWEEN YOUR MIDDLE AND RING FINGERS?

YES - This means you like privacy. You are also resourceful and are quite content to do things quietly on your own.

NO - This means you're a home-loving person and like the security of having people you love around you.

IS THERE...

A WIDE SPACE BETWEEN YOUR RING AND LITTLE FINGERS?

YES - This means you hate being tied down. Freedom is important to you and the thing you would loathe above everything else would be to be put in prison.

NO - This means you like things to stay the same. You tend to be unsure of yourself and of your abilities and need the support of a best friend.

Are your fingers

Think back to when you were working out the four different hand shapes, and to the second rule you learned which was to judge whether the fingers are long or short. You may remember that short fingers are part of the Earth and Fire hands, and long fingers belong to the Air and Water hands. The actual length of the fingers can tell you a lot about a person.

Short fingers

People whose fingers are much shorter than their palms are quick but impatient. They don't like to hang around and may take short cuts to get things done fast. They are quick

SHORT or LONG?

learners and only need to be shown how to do something once. However, don't expect them to pore over finicky details, because that's what they hate most. They much prefer taking a wider view of any situation, making grand plans, or organizing people and events. Once short-fingered people have set the ball in motion, they're happy to leave others to cross all the t's and dot all the i's. This leaves them free to do what they're best at - which is to make new grand plans and start on the next project they have in mind. If you have long fingers, you probably get annoyed with short-fingered people because, in your opinion, they simply don't pay enough attention to detail.

Long fingers

People with long fingers are patient and like to take their time to get things right. They have a sharp eye for detail and can spend hours concentrating on intricate work such as drawing miniature pictures that can only be seen properly through a magnifying glass, or sewing tiny cross-stitch embroideries that are about the size of a postage stamp. These people have tidy minds and careful hands and, unlike short-fingered folk, they don't get fed up easily or give up on jobs that need lots of attention to get things exactly right. If you have short fingers you probably think that long-fingered people fiddle and fuss far too much over trivial things. As far as they're concerned, however, they like to be precise and they want to get things just so.

Fingers and Fables

For thousands of years the fingers have been called by the same mythological names as the mounts at the top of the palm.

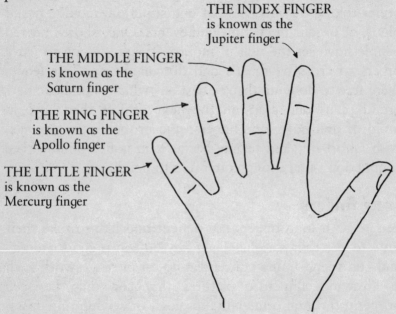

THE INDEX FINGER is known as the Jupiter finger

THE MIDDLE FINGER is known as the Saturn finger

THE RING FINGER is known as the Apollo finger

THE LITTLE FINGER is known as the Mercury finger

Like the mounts, each finger represents an area of your life and, depending on its length and appearance, it can reveal a lot about how you behave, what you think is important in life, what you're good at, and what you find most interesting to do. To a hand reader, each name is like a shorthand description of what that finger represents.

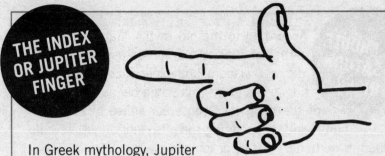

THE INDEX
OR JUPITER
FINGER

In Greek mythology, Jupiter was the chief god and ruler of the world. His name was given to this particular finger because it represents leadership, how you see yourself in the world and whether you think that other people respect you and listen to what you have to say.

The index is the "me" finger. It's the one we use to point with and if you watch people putting up their hands to answer a question, you may see that many hold up their Jupiter fingers as if they're saying, "Me, pick me. I know the answer."

Length

It's best when this finger is roughly the same length as your ring finger, as this means that you are confident about your abilities and happy with the way you are. If it is very long, however, it means that you like being in control and others may think you're a bit bossy. People whose Jupiter finger is very much shorter than their ring finger tend to be shy and unsure of themselves. Very short Jupiter fingers are seen on people who are described as having a chip on their shoulder.

THE MIDDLE OR SATURN FINGER

According to the old myths, Saturn was the father of Jupiter and so was associated with old age, wisdom, and experience. The middle finger was given this name because this area of the hand represents our sense of responsibility and, depending on its length, it reveals whether we behave wisely or foolishly.

Length

A good length for the middle finger is to be slightly longer than the ring finger. If yours is like that, it means you're sensible and reliable. This sort of finger tells you that you have a healthy attitude to your responsibilities and that you carry out your duties in a mature fashion. When this finger is noticeably short, however, it reveals an immature person who runs away from responsibility. It's very difficult to rely on someone with a very short Saturn finger. In contrast, when this finger is much longer than the ring finger, it shows there is too much seriousness is that person's nature. A very long middle finger reveals a person who is too self-absorbed, can't take a joke, and only sees the miserable side of life. You can tell these people a mile off because they grumble about everything all the time. They're what you might call moaning minnies.

Black Clou

Alway Moa mi

THE RING OR APOLLO FINGER

In the myths, Apollo drove the sun across the skies in a golden chariot. This means that Apollo was the god who was responsible for bringing light to the world after the darkness of the night. The sun, of course, brings us warmth, too. It cheers us up and makes us feel better, so it's appropriate that this finger should be named after Apollo because it represents our sense of happiness, the lighter side of life, and our ability to make and appreciate beautiful things.

Length

If your Apollo finger is roughly as long as your index finger, you have the ideal length for this finger. It shows you are a happy person who is good at arts and crafts and enjoys music and dancing. In fact, you're good fun to be with. Someone whose Apollo finger is very long tends to live in a fantasy world, day-dreaming of fame, wealth, and success. If it's very short, it means the person is not especially creative, so his or her talents will lie elsewhere.

THE LITTLE OR MERCURY FINGER

Mercury was the messenger of the gods. As this finger deals with communication and the speed at which our minds work, it is a very suitable name to give to this finger. Mercury was a busy god. As well as taking messages to and fro, he was also known as the bringer of good fortune, the giver of sleep, and the god who led men astray. What a lot of associations for the smallest finger of the hand!

Length

This finger will usually be shorter than the rest. The best way to find out its true length is to measure it from its tip down to the crease where it joins the palm, then compare this measurement against the ring finger. Don't try to compare them side by side on the hand because the little finger is often set low into the palm - sometimes it is as much as a centimeter lower than the ring finger - so a side-by-side comparison won't give you an accurate reading.

A normal-sized Mercury finger will reach just beyond the top crease line of the nail section of the ring finger. If yours is like this, it shows that you've got a lively mind and a good ability with languages. A long Mercury finger reaching quite far up that top section of the ring finger reveals a person who is clever and witty. People with long little fingers are good at speaking and can be excellent writers. Long Mercury fingers can also be a sign that the person is

good at sciences or has the ability to make lots of money. A short Mercury finger won't reach as far as the top crease on the ring finger and this can mean that the person finds it difficult to put his or her thoughts into words.

Interestingly, many little fingers have a tip that bends slightly towards the ring finger. This shows a sharp, shrewd, and quick-witted mentality. But if you ever see a very crooked little finger, beware! It can mean that its owner doesn't always stick to the truth. Remember, Mercury was the god who led men astray.

A word of caution, however. Not every crooked little finger reveals a dishonest person! The finger may have been bent in an accident or distorted by rheumatism - a disease that attacks the joints of the bones. A good hand analyst never makes a judgement before carefully checking all the facts.

WHAT'S IN

The Ancient Romans were an earthy lot of people. They enjoyed all sorts of bodily pleasures and weren't at all embarrassed to talk about these things openly. For them, going to the lavatory and washing themselves - even the most intimate parts of their bodies - were such natural, everyday activities that they didn't bat an eyelid if they had to do these things in public. After all, they had communal baths and rows of communal toilets!

It's not at all surprising, therefore, that the names they gave to the fingers described the function that each finger was best at performing.

The Romans gave the name **index** to the first or forefinger, because this meant the pointer. Certainly, whenever we want to indicate something, it's the most natural thing in the world to stretch out our forefingers and point with them. Pointing with any other finger feels quite uncomfortable, don't you think?

The middle finger takes us into slightly embarrassing territory. You see, the Romans had two names for this finger. They called it the **obscoenus** or the **impudicus**, meaning the rude or unclean finger. The reason for this is that they used the middle finger to clean themselves after they had been to the lavatory. This may embarrass us, but of course it didn't embarrass the Romans.

The other reason for the names is that this finger was used, and still is to this day, for a very rude gesture. Perhaps you've seen it - it's quite a favorite among angry

A NAME?

motorists. It's the one where the fist is clenched and the middle finger is extended and jabbed sharply up into the air. It's not a gesture that is recommended because it is so obscene - precisely the word the Romans gave to this finger.

Now, have you ever noticed how hard it is to move the ring finger on its own? It's almost impossible to hold it up straight without moving the fingers on either side of it. Because it doesn't move independently, it's thought to be the weakest finger in the hand and therefore it's not used on its own when we clean, groom or wash ourselves. For this reason the Romans considered the ring finger to be the cleanest finger in the hand, so it was the one that doctors and apothecaries (the people who made the medicines) used for stirring their lotions and potions. This is why the Romans called the ring finger the **digitus medicus**, meaning the doctor's finger.

When it comes to the little finger, we're back to grooming again. The Romans called this finger the **auricularis**, a term meaning the ear. No prizes for guessing why it was given this name - it is, of course, the only finger that will fit comfortably into your ear, for whatever reason...

Finger Phalanges

A phalange is the name given to the little bones that make up the fingers. Each finger has three phalanges, also known as the base, middle, and nail sections. Depending on its length, how it looks and which finger it belongs to, each section tells us something about how we use our talents.

On your outline, draw in three divisions on each finger - the first at the base where the finger meets the palm, the next a third of the way up, and the last another third of the way up from there. Now take a ruler and measure each of the twelve phalanges on your fingers. Start from the very tip of each finger down to the first joint line, then from that joint line down to the next one, and from that one down to the lowest joint line at the top of the palm. Write the measurements down on the outline, inside each finger division.

Which of the three sets of phalanges in your hand are the longest - those at the top, in the middle, or at the base of the fingers? And which are the shortest?

The top phalanges

If your top phalanges tend to be longer than your middle or basal ones it means that you are a thinker. Long top phalanges belong to people who like studying, are good at academic subjects at school, and really enjoy looking up facts when they have a project to do. They're not necessarily very practical people, however. For example, someone with long top phalanges may know everything there is

THE TOP OR NAIL PHALANGES DESCRIBE HOW YOUR MIND WORKS

THE MIDDLE PHALANGES INDICATE HOW PRACTICAL YOU ARE

THE BASE PHALANGES REVEAL YOUR PHYSICAL NEEDS AND DESIRES

to know about art and artists, but if it came to actually painting a portrait, he or she may be completely useless.

If your top phalanges are not the longest sections of your fingers, it means that while you probably cope very well with your lessons, learning and fact-finding may not be at the top of your list of favorite pursuits. Look at the next two sets to find out which areas you personally excel in.

The middle phalanges

If your middle phalanges are the longest of the three sets, you're a terrific organizer and you're brilliant at sorting out people and problems. Because you're so capable and able to find a practical solution to every situation, you'll probably make a success of whatever you choose to do in life. People who have a good head for business and are efficient workers often have long middle sections to their fingers. They're very good at presenting their work neatly and getting it done on time with little fuss. They're also brilliant at managing money.

If your middle phalanges are the shortest, you could try to take a more practical approach - aim to be a little tidier and more disciplined in your work.

The basal phalanges

If the longest phalanges in your hand are the basal ones, you're likely to be a very physical sort of person. People with long sections here love rolling up their sleeves and getting stuck in. They're often hard working and don't mind getting their hands dirty. Many of them excel in sports and make a very good career for themselves in that line. But the most glorious thing about these people is that they have a tremendous appreciation of the good things in life. For example, they might adore cooking and eating food. In fact, some of the most brilliant chefs and owners of high-class restaurants have these long or well-developed basal sections. Alternatively, they might be lovers of beautiful things such as paintings, jewelery, or antiques, and become famous collectors.

If, however, your basal phalanges are short, it could mean that you're not a particularly physically active sort of person, or that material things aren't important to your happiness.

Rings on Your Fingers

If you look closely at old paintings and photographs, you will see that ordinary people didn't wear many rings in the past. A woman might have worn a wedding or engagement ring on her third finger. A man might have worn a wedding ring and possibly a signet ring on his little finger. These days, however, both men and women often cram as many rings as they can onto their fingers and thumbs!

People wear rings for different reasons. Wedding rings, engagement rings, and friendship rings are all tokens of love. A grand ring can be a status symbol - it shows how rich or important you are. Other rings are worn simply for decoration, to follow fashion or to draw the eye to beautiful hands.

Whatever the reason a person might wear a ring, the important thing for a hand reader to note is which finger the ring is worn on, as this will reveal clues about that person's most secret feelings.

Anyone who finds wearing a ring on the index finger comfortable could be rather vain as well as a bit pushy. Remember, this is the me, me, me finger!

Those who wear a ring on their middle fingers tend to be materialistic - they like to have money and possessions.

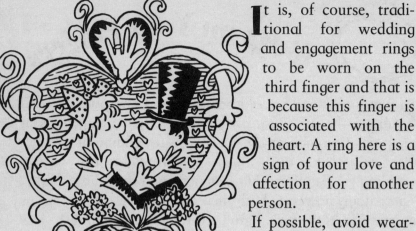

It is, of course, traditional for wedding and engagement rings to be worn on the third finger and that is because this finger is associated with the heart. A ring here is a sign of your love and affection for another person.

If possible, avoid wearing a ring on your little finger. This finger represents our ability to communicate and it's thought that people who wear a ring here are subconsciously (without being aware of it) saying that they have trouble expressing their feelings. This means they may find it difficult to make or keep friends. If you know someone whose relationships are always going wrong and that person wears a little-finger ring, you could suggest that he or she removes it, to see if that improves matters. You never know - it might just do the trick!

Finally, a ring on the thumb could be a sign of a stubborn and willful person. These people will expect you to back down long before they do. Next time you're in an art gallery, look at the portraits of powerful people from the past to confirm this theory.

The Importance of the Thumb

Many people would agree that the thumb is the most important part of the hand. Because it can be moved into a position where it can face the other fingers, we can hold, grip and use tools with amazing precision. If we did not have thumbs, we would find it very difficult to pick things up, fend for ourselves, or make things, so it would be really hard to turn our thoughts and ideas into reality.

Here's an experiment for you to try. Tuck your thumbs tight into your palms. Now, using only your four fingers, see if you can do any of the things listed in the box.

How successful were you? Normally you would carry out these simple tasks without a second thought. Trying to do them without a thumb, however, helps you to understand how important the thumb has been in human evolution. It is partly because of the thumb that human beings have evolved so far ahead of all the other animals on Earth.

- DO UP YOUR BUTTONS
- TIE YOUR SHOE LACES
- TURN THE DOOR KNOB SO YOU CAN GET OUT OF THE ROOM
- HOLD A KNIFE AND TRY TO CUT UP YOUR FOOD
- PICK UP A HAIR BRUSH AND BRUSH YOUR HAIR
- GET DRESSED OR UNDRESSED
- UNSCREW A JAR OF PEANUT BUTTER
- WRITE YOUR NAME AND ADDRESS

The thumb is just as important when it comes to reading hands. It is vital to pay a lot of attention to the shape and size of the thumb on a person's hand, because this will tell you a great deal about that person. For example, you can tell whether a person is weak or strong, understanding or insensitive, easily influenced or stubborn as a mule, and lots more.

This may sound silly, but a thumb should look as if it "belongs" to the rest of the hand. This means that if the hand is long and thin, the thumb should be long and thin, too. If the hand is short and solid, the thumb should also be short and solid. But a long thin thumb on a short, thick hand would look completely out of keeping. Likewise, a short, stubby thumb on a long, elegant hand would look quite unbalanced. And that is the key: the shape and size of the thumb must balance the shape and size of the rest of the hand.

This is something you must judge for yourself when you look at a hand. When you have studied a few, you'll easily be able to spot if a hand looks well balanced or not.

Our thumbs reveal a lot about our strength of character. No matter what brilliant talents you may discover in a palm or in the fingers, if the thumb is weak it means that person will not have enough oomph to make a success of those abilities. Alternatively, even if only a couple of talents are shown in a palm, when the thumb is good and strong, that person possesses enough energy and drive to work hard on those limited abilities and become really successful with them.

What Does Your Thumb Say About You?

Like the fingers, the thumb is made up of phalanges. Also like the fingers, it's made up of three sections, but we can only see two of them because the third one is embedded in the palm under the mount of Venus. So, to all intents and purposes, when we talk about the thumb, we refer only to the first phalange (which is the top or nail section), and the second phalange (which joins onto the palm).

The top phalange represents your strength of will.
The second phalange represents your powers of logic and reasoning.

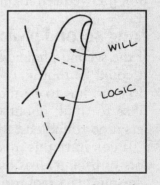

Measure your thumb from the tip down to the first crease line and write that measurement down on your outline. Then measure the second section from the top crease line to the line where the thumb meets the palm. Jot that measurement down too, and draw in the crease lines.

Ideally, both phalanges should be roughly the same length. If they are, it means you're a well-balanced, level-headed person who is able to make logical decisions based on common sense.

Long top phalanges

If the top phalange is much longer than the second section, it means you're very strong-minded. While that is good because it gives you the power to see things through, at times you may not want to listen to reason. There's an expression that aptly describes this: you cut off your nose to spite your face.

If you do possess a top section that is very much longer than the second one, try to think twice before you put your foot down in any situation. Ask yourself, whenever you have to make an important decision, whether or not you have looked at the problem from every angle. Is it possible that you've been taking a rather biased view?

Long second phalanges

If the second phalange is much longer than the top section, it could be that you tend to shilly-shally too much when a decision has to be made. This is the sign of someone who likes to think about every aspect of a problem, and who lets it go round and round in his or her mind.

If you have this type of thumb it can mean that you have lots of brainy ideas but you find it difficult to come to conclusions. The real problem is that you have too many ideas - they crowd into your mind and confuse you. Basically, it means you end up not seeing the wood for the trees. What you need to do is to take a deep breath and a step back and think which ideas won't work because they are weak, silly or impractical. Throw these ideas out, then look at the ideas you're left with. Write them down on a sheet of paper and pin them up on your wall. Treat them like New Year resolutions and work at them until you get the results you want.

THE ANGLE OF THE THUMB

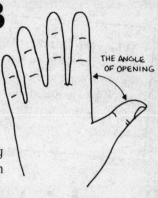

THE ANGLE
OF OPENING

Go back to the outline you drew around your hand and take a look at the angle the thumb forms to the palm. Does the thumb lie close to the index finger, forming a tight angle? Does it lie between 45-90 degrees away from the index? Or does it stretch even wider than 90 degrees? This angle is very significant. **Read on...**

When the thumb forms a tight angle to the palm

If you have this formation you are able to concentrate on your work for a long time without being distracted. Emotionally, you tend to keep your feelings to yourself. This is known as playing your cards close to your chest. It means that other people can't tell what you're thinking. If you find you hold your thumbs like this, you could consider taking up a new hobby - something a bit different from your usual activities. You'd be surprised how much a new interest will open up your mind and give you lots of new things to think about.

When the thumb forms a 45-90 degree angle to the palm

This is a fairly normal angle and shows a good deal of common sense. If this is how you usually hold your thumb, it means you're fair and open-minded. It also suggests that you're tolerant and flexible. You can take a change of situations, meetings with new people, and unexpected events in your stride. You go with the flow, but you also know when enough's enough.

> ### When the thumb forms a very wide angle to the palm
> Does your thumb lie further than 90 degrees away from your index finger? If so, it means you are a very laid back sort of person. You can be rather extravagant and dramatic, possibly a bit of a show-off, and you're especially prone to going over the top. You're lively and great fun to be with, but you must learn when to apply the brakes!

Bony Joints

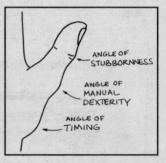

ANGLE OF
STUBBORNNESS

ANGLE OF
MANUAL
DEXTERITY

ANGLE OF
TIMING

Look at the outline of your thumb. Follow its shape along the outside from the tip down towards the wrist. Does the bony joint at the top crease stick out? If it does, it means you're stubborn. The more it juts out the more obstinate you can be. If you have this formation, it's almost impossible to get you to change your mind once you have dug in your heels!

Trace down to the next joint where the base of the thumb meets the palm. If this sticks out sharply it means you are very creative with your hands. This formation is called "the angle of manual dexterity." People who are brilliant at making things and enjoy do-it-yourself or handicrafts very often have a sharp angle here.

Follow down from the thumb to where the palm meets the wrist. Whenever you see a sharp angle at this point, it means that the person has a wonderful ear for music.

Many musicians have this formation in their hands. It's actually known as "the angle of timing."

If you have this angularity but still insist you can't string two notes together, it can mean that you have an exquisite sense of timing rather than being musical. Sometimes brilliant sportsmen and women, who can't sing for toffee but who know just when to hit the ball to get it into the net, have this marking. Comedians, too, often have this construction in their hands. Like sporting types, they may not be brilliant musicians but their great sense of timing enables them to drop the punch line at exactly the right moment to make their audience split their sides with laughter.

The Nails

Do you bite your nails? Lots of people do and they are sometimes too embarrassed to let you have a close look at their hands. You can reassure them, however, that hand readers don't look at the white manicured tip of the nail. What we're interested in is the pink growing part that's attached to the finger. Problems only arise if chewing has distorted the shape of the nail. If this has happened, you'll just have to do your best to work out what the nail is really like, or you could skip this section altogether. The good news, though, is that when people manage to stop nibbling, the nails soon go back to their natural shape.

How the nails are formed

The nails never stop growing. Whether you're awake or asleep, nail production just keeps on going full steam ahead. Think of the nail as a conveyor belt. It's made deep in the tissue beneath the skin and rolls out past the cuticle and over the nail bed to the tip of the finger.

It takes about six months for the nail to grow from cuticle to tip. Interestingly, our nails grow faster in the summer than in the winter. Our fingernails grow faster than our toenails, and the nails on the dominant hand grow faster than those on the passive hand.

A record of events

GROOVE

Sometimes you find a little horizontal groove in a nail. This can be the result of an accident - for example, if you have shut your finger in a door.

When these grooves occur on all the nails, however, it means that something happened at some point that affected the actual production of the nail. It's as if there was a hiccup in the manufacturing process, causing a fault to develop in the nice smooth sheets of nail.

What might have caused this hiccup in the system? It could be shock. If, for example, you have received really bad news or you have been involved in a serious accident, it may be recorded in your nails. Another thing that can upset nail production is going on a sudden crash diet. This is because nothing affects the nails more dramatically than poor nutrition. In fact, if you don't eat a balanced diet, or if you're allergic to certain foods, your nails will suffer.

Whether it's damage to one nail, or grooves across all the nails, these marks can tell you when the trauma (the upset to your system) took place. As a matter of fact, you can date that event quite closely.

As we know that a nail takes six months to grow from cuticle to tip (and we're only considering the pink part, remember, not the white tip), we can be certain that a groove in the centre of the nail must have occurred about three months ago. A groove nearer the top would mean that the event took place about five to six months ago. If, however, the mark is at the bottom, just past the cuticle, the upset must have been recent because this part of the nail has only just been formed.

A word of advice here. If someone's nails reveal a lot of horizontal grooves, go gently when discussing the causes - you don't want to give the person any further distress.

Nails of All Shapes

Fingernails come in a variety of shapes. Some are square, some are broad, some are fan-shaped and some look like almonds. Again, when you're judging the shape of the nail, only look at the pink part. Incidentally, this is known as the "quick" or living part of the nail. Each shape reveals some interesting information about its owner.

The square nail

Square nails are as high as they are wide and they can be small or large. People with this type of nail tend to be solid, sensible, and well balanced – the sort of people who take things in their stride. The larger the square, the more even-tempered the person will be. Very small square nails can reveal someone who is highly critical or gets irritable quickly. But when you're judging size, you must take into account the size of the hand. Small nails on a small hand are not small nails at all – they are average nails. The term small only applies when there are small nails on a large hand.

The fan-shaped nail

These nails are triangular in shape and look like a fan that has been opened out. They reveal a delicate nervous system and are seen on the hands of people who worry a lot, or who find life stressful. Lots of rest, exercise and fresh air works wonders for owners of fan-shaped nails.

The broad nail

Broad nails are usually found only on the thumbs. You can tell a broad nail because it is much wider than it is high. People with these thumb nails can have sudden flashes of temper. They might not fly off the handle very often, but when they do it's like a volcanic eruption!

The almond shaped nail

People who have these lovely shaped nails are often gentle and dreamy. They are not the strongest of people, certainly not as robust as those with square nails, but they have an easy-going, kind nature and usually show consideration to others.

The Moons

The moons are the semicircular areas of the nails at the base near the cuticle. The technical name for the moon is the lunule. The color and size of the moons can tell us a lot about a person's health. The best moons are milky-white and are visible on each nail. People whose moons have a bluish tinge may not be getting enough oxygen into their bodies. Perhaps they're not very fit and could do with some gentle exercise. People with no moons at all tend to be sensitive and may also be nervous.

3 MAKING PRINTS

Every single fingerprint is unique. If you searched across the whole wide world you would still not find two that are exactly the same. Even identical twins have different fingerprints, and those on your right hand do not match those on your left hand.

We inherit our fingerprints, which means that the patterns on your fingers are likely to be the same type as those on your mother's or your father's fingers. If they're not similar to your parents' prints, they may resemble those of a grandparent. When you find out whose fingerprints are like yours, you'll discover which member of your family you take after.

From the moment they appear on our tiny unborn fingers in around the third month of our development in the womb, our fingerprints never change. They grow as we grow, but not a single line of the patterns ever alters throughout our lives. We can cut our fingers, we can file them down with an emery board, we can even try to burn the fingerprints off. It doesn't matter what we do to them - our fingerprint patterns will grow back exactly the same as before. Every line, every groove will be just as it was.

But of course you already know that everybody's fingerprints are unique because you've watched all those detective films on television. You've seen the murderer being tracked down because he inadvertently left his prints on the whisky glass at the scene of the crime.

Although these days we all know about the uniqueness of the patterns on our fingertips, in terms of recent history we've only known about this for the last hundred years. The strange thing is that the Chinese emperors knew that no two fingerprints are alike as far back as 3000 BC. The people of ancient India had this knowledge too. Official documents dating back to those times were "signed," not with names, but with a thumbprint. Obviously, back then, everybody knew that each of those thumb prints could only have been made by one particular person.

Somehow or other, between then and the late 19th century, we forgot that we all possess these unique identification marks on the end of our fingers. It wasn't until two separate incidents took place, thousands of miles apart, that the world rediscovered this vitally important piece of knowledge.

What happened was that a missionary doctor, working in the Far East during the 1890s made a surprising discovery. He used to spend his free time digging for archaeological remains and was puzzled because he kept finding bits of ancient pots that had fingerprints pressed into them. For a while he pondered on the meaning of this and then it hit him like a blinding flash of lightning - the fingerprints must have been the signatures of the potters.

At the very same time a government inspector in India,

who was in charge of supervising the wages of plantation workers, noticed how the workers "signed" for their money. Instead of using their names, they pressed their thumbs into ink and then onto the payment ledgers. He thought about this for a while and then realized that everyone's fingerprints must be different. In fact, identifying people by their thumbprints is actually much safer than using signatures, since no one can fake their fingerprints!

Fingerprints make history

News of these two discoveries soon reached the police force back in England. This was brilliant timing because Scotland Yard had been desperately searching for a foolproof way of identifying criminals. Immediately, they set up a department to look into the whole business. They collected thousands and thousands of prints and compared each one until they were satisfied that every person's fingerprints are indeed unique.

When, in 1902, Scotland Yard detectives found a fingerprint in some tacky paint at the scene of a robbery, they were able to prove in court that it belonged to the chief suspect, Harry Jackson.

Jackson's conviction for theft was the first court case in which fingerprints were used as evidence, so it made fingerprinting history. From that time on, fingerprinting revolutionized police work, not only for the detectives at Scotland Yard, but for police officers all over the world.

Examining your fingerprints

If you look closely at the skin on your fingertips, you'll notice that it looks a bit like sheets of corrugated iron because it's made up of rows of high ridges and deep grooves. In some places these ridges and grooves run in straight parallel lines, then suddenly they may swirl about and sweep into patterns that loop and circle around the ends of your fingers.

These patterns are grouped into six different types. This is what they look like:

| LOOP | WHORL | ARCH | TENTED ARCH | DOUBLE LOOP | PEACOCK'S EYE |

To find out which patterns you possess, you need to examine your fingertips under a strong light, or better still, use a magnifying glass.

Some people have the same pattern on all their fingertips. Others have a mixture. It all depends on whose patterns you have inherited.

Each pattern tells you something about your character. Count up how many of each type you have. The pattern that appears most often will indicate what you're most like, but you should also take into account the other patterns on your fingers, as you'll have a small percentage of those personality characteristics in you too.

For instance, seven loops and three whorls means you're mostly a "loop" type of person, but you also have touches of the "whorl" character. However, if you have five loops and five whorls, you are a fifty-fifty mixture of both types.

The Loop

What it looks like: A loop is quite easy to spot because the ridges curl around to form a hairpin bend.

What it says about you: If most of your patterns are loops it means you're a flexible and adaptable sort of person, someone who is open-minded and happy to go along with other people's wishes. Being part of a group is important to you and you enjoy chatting to your friends, exchanging news and gossip about other people and what's going on in your world. At school, you're good at creative subjects. You like languages and literature, word games and working on the computer.

The Whorl

What it looks like: There are two forms of whorl pattern. In one, the ridge lines go round and round in a spiral. In the other, the ridges form a set of neat little rings, one inside the other.

What it says about you: If most of your fingerprints are whorls it means you like to think long and hard about things. It's no good people expecting you to make up your mind in an instant, you don't work like that. You need to mull things over in your mind. You're a very responsible sort of person and prefer to take charge. This means you're happier when you're the leader, rather than when you have to follow others. Once you've made up your mind, it takes a lot to make you change your views and opinions.

The Arch

What it looks like: On some hands this pattern can look a bit like a humpback bridge. It's rare to find arches on all the fingers. Usually, they only occur on the thumbs and index fingers.

What it says about you: Even just two or three arches show that you have a practical, sensible, and down-to-earth attitude to life. If you have this pattern you probably excel at anything constructive and your logical mind enables you to solve problems in ways that others can only admire. You are also always ready to help others. You may be shy and find it hard to talk about your innermost feelings, but you are realistic and you have your feet firmly on the ground.

The Tented Arch

What it looks like: This pattern looks like a steeper arch, with a center line through the middle rather like a tent pole holding up a tent. You're unlikely to have more than two or three of these.

What it says about you: If you have this pattern it means you get very excited and enthusiastic about new ideas. In fact, you can be so caught up in your latest interest that you get quite carried away. The more projects you have on the go at any one time, the happier you are - although this doesn't necessarily mean that you'll get round to finishing them all!

The Double Loop

What it looks like: This pattern is made up of two entwined loops that swirl around each other, forming an "S" shape. You usually find it only on the thumbs and index fingers.

What it says about you: Look at these two loops and you'll see how they appear to be pulling in opposite directions. If you possess this pattern, that just about sums you up - you find it hard to make up your mind. It's the "Will I? Won't I?" pattern. On the positive side, you like to look at a problem from all angles and you're brilliant at seeing everybody else's point of view. This makes you a terrific judge of people and situations.

The Peacock's Eye

What it looks like: You won't find many of these patterns in a hand. When they are present, they are usually only on the little or ring fingers.

What it says about you: If you have a peacock's eye pattern in your hand, consider yourself very lucky because this is the

mark of good fortune. Perhaps you'll win raffle prizes; perhaps you'll get picked at the audition; perhaps you'll have an amazingly miraculous escape. Whatever happens, you seem to have Lady Luck on your side.

Palmar Patterns

Not many people realize that you can find patterns on your palms that are similar to those on your fingertips.

If you look very closely at your own palm, you'll be able to make out the ridges and grooves on the surface of your skin. Mostly, these ridges and grooves sweep around in parallel rows, but sometimes they swirl themselves into a pattern like a fingerprint.

These "palmar patterns" are very often formed into loops. Although you may occasionally come across some of the other patterns, they are much more rare in the palm.

The most common place to find these loops is at the very top of the palm, dropping down from the webbing between the fingers. Now and again, however, you may come across some on the mounts of Venus and Luna, too.

Some people have several of these loops. Others may have only one. Still others have none at all. Examine your palm very carefully to see if you have any and then read on to find out what they mean.

A palm loop between the thumb and index finger

This pattern is very rare, but if you do have one it means you have masses of courage.

A palm loop between the index and middle fingers

This is another rare pattern. It is known as the "Loop of the Rajah" because it was thought to be the mark of nobility. Strangely enough, some people who possess this loop have actually been able to trace their ancestry back to a royal line. These days, however, we tend to interpret this loop as signifying "executive abilities," which means that the person has good leadership or managerial qualities.

A palm loop between the middle and ring fingers

This pattern is known as the "Loop of Vocation." If you have one of these it means you love helping people. It's often seen in the hands of doctors and carers, and other people who devote themselves to working for the welfare of others.

A palm loop between the middle and little fingers

This pattern is known as the "Loop of Humour." Those who possess it tend to have a rather odd sense of humour - they laugh at situations that most people don't find funny at all. The best thing about these people is that they don't take themselves too seriously, so they're always ready to laugh at themselves when they make mistakes.

Palmar patterns on the mount of Venus

Skin patterns here often reveal musical talents or simply a strong appreciation of music. On some hands you may find a loop in this area or, more rarely, a whorl. The whorl here is known as a Bee String and reveals a particular love of the music of stringed instruments.

Palmar patterns on the mount of Luna

The majority of hands have no specific markings here, but when they do occur they can take several forms. A long loop that enters the palm from the percussion edge and lies across the mount is known as the "loop of flora and fauna." It is found in the hands of people who have a special understanding of plants and animals. A loop that enters from the wrist and sweeps upwards into the palm is known as the "loop of inspiration." This pattern is extremely rare. It is found in the hands of people with exceptional artistic or poetic talents. A loop that sweeps down from the center of the palm, looking rather like a teardrop, is called the "Loop of Water." It is found in the hands of people who are, in one way or another, drawn to water. Either they have a passion for water sports, or they live (or would love to live) near a river or by the sea.

MUSIC WHORL ON VENUS MOUNT

WATER LOOP

FLORA & FAUNA LOOP

ARTISTIC OR POETIC LOOP

Putting it Down on Paper

Did you find it difficult to see your palmar patterns? One traditional solution is to take a hand print. If this is done well it will show up the fine lines all over your hand. You've probably done this before, most likely at preschool where you made splodgy hand print patterns which your mother proudly put up on the kitchen wall.

Splodgy patterns are definitely not what you want here, however! To read the lines on your hands you need good, clear hand prints, and that may take several goes before you get it right. You'll also need some basic equipment, and if you can get a friend to help you, so much the better. By the way, if someone does offer to help you, make sure you take their hand prints at the same time. Never miss the opportunity to take the prints of any willing guinea pig who may be around - you need to build up a collection of different prints to get as much experience as possible of reading hands, so the more you can get, the merrier.

Preparing to take a print

Professional hand analysts use tubes of water-soluble lino printing ink which are not too expensive and can be bought from most art shops. One tube will be enough for at least a hundred prints! Make sure it is water-soluble because then you can simply wash it off with soap and water, and if you get any ink on the table or the door handle you can easily wipe it off with a damp cloth. Steer clear of inks that are not water-soluble. You need special solvents to get them off your hands and they can be very messy to use.

Water-soluble lino printing ink comes in various colors, although black is the traditional one to use. However, there are no set rules about this, so if you want purple or lime-green hand prints, that's fine!

If you can't wait until the shops open and you want to get started straight away, you could use lipstick instead. You will need to find a strong, dark color, such as deep red, crimson, or even black! Light pinks don't generally give satisfactory results. The only problem with using lipstick is that it stays greasy and sticky for a long time, so you could smudge the prints when you're measuring them. Nevertheless, lipstick is a very useful stand-by.

As well as the ink, you will need to gather together a few more items before you begin. You'll find the list of equipment and instructions for taking high-quality hand prints on pages 76-77.

EQUIPMENT

- Water-soluble lino printing ink, or lipstick
- A pad or sheets of plain paper - preferably A4 size
- A sharp pencil
- A pen
- A printer's roller, or a rolling pin covered in cling film
- A pastry board (covered in foil), or a glossy magazine cover
- A table knife
- Some tissues

Taking a

If you're using lipstick, lightly rub it all over your palm and fingers in the same way. You need only a very light covering as too much lipstick will make a splodgy mess.

Make sure the center of the palm, and the edges of the hand, fingers, and thumb, are all coated with ink or lipstick. Shake your hand in the air to relax it a little, then place it comfortably on the paper.

STEP 1

Squeeze a tiny blob of ink (about the size of a fat peanut) onto the foil-covered board or glossy magazine cover, and roll it out thinly with the printer's roller or the rolling pin. When the roller is covered in ink, roll it evenly all over your palm, fingers and thumb, stopping about 1.5 centimeters below the crease line where the palm joins the wrist.

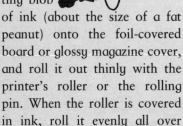

STEP 2

Now, without moving your hand, take the pencil and draw right round the outline. Start at the wrist and trace around the thumb and fingers then down the outer edge, ending up on the opposite side of the wrist.

h a n d   p r i n t

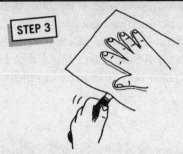

STEP 3

thumb and each finger onto the bottom of the paper, in a neat row.

STEP 5

Take several copies of each hand in this way and put the date in the top right-hand corner of each sheet of paper. Three other essential pieces of information that you must write below the date on each sheet are:

Still keeping your hand firmly on the paper, slip the blade of the knife under the paper and press up into the hollow of your palm. Slide the knife around a bit just to make sure the whole of the palm comes into contact with the paper. Now, carefully peel your hand away.

• the name of the person whose hand this is
• his/her date of birth
• whether the person is right-handed or left-handed.

STEP 4

At this stage, put a little more ink (using the roller) or lipstick all over your fingertips and, one by one, press the tip of your

NB Keeping careful records right from the start is very important. Add the data instantly every time, or you'll end up not knowing who on earth the prints belong to or when they were made.

A Cleaner Alternative to Taking Hand Prints

Taking a photocopy of your hands can be a useful alternative to an inked print - and a much less messy business as well! If either of your parents has access to a photocopier, perhaps you could ask them if you can use it to take your prints. Also ask them to take some copies of their own hands for your collection. Adults won't mind that so much because it's quick and clean. Remember, the more examples of hands you can collect, the better.

But don't get confused!

There's a big difference between studying a hand print and a photocopy of a hand - even the professionals have to stop and think for a minute to get it right. You see, when you look at a hand print, it is a mirror image of the hand. If you take an ink print of your right hand, for example, the thumb on the paper is pointing to the left. However, when you lift your hand off the paper and look at your own up-turned palm, you'll see that your right-hand thumb is pointing to the right.

In contrast, when you take a photocopy of your hand, it is a photograph - not a mirror image - so your right-hand thumb is pointing to the right, just as it does when you turn your real hand over to look at your palm.

This can be quite mind-boggling at first! The best advice is to jot down on the paper whether the hand is the right or left one immediately after you've taken the print or photocopy. Just write R or L in the top left-hand corner, then you'll know which hand you're looking at when you come to study it later on.

ADDING TO YOUR COLLECTION

Newspapers and magazines are very useful sources of examples of hands for your collection. Keep a lookout for pictures of film and pop stars waving their hands. You can tell a lot about the celebrity from these shots because they can show you quite clearly the shape of the palm, the length of the fingers and the angle of the thumb. Just occasionally the photo can be so sharp that you can even see the lines in the palm.

Right Hand
vs
Left Hand

Are you right-handed or left-handed? For a hand reader, this is a very important question because each hand contains different information.

The hand that you use most is called the "dominant" hand, while the other one is referred to as the "passive" hand. So, for a right-handed person, the right hand is dominant and the left hand is passive. Likewise, for a left-handed person the left hand is dominant and the right hand is passive.

Very often you can tell which is which because the dominant hand appears stronger and more developed. Also, the lines in the palm of the dominant hand are usually clearer and stand out more.

The dominant hand reveals how you develop your talents. It shows how you behave in public, and how you come across to other people. The lines here reveal what a person is like as an adult and they register events that happen during that person's lifetime. You could describe this hand as revealing the *outer* you.

The passive hand tells us about the gifts and talents that you are born with. This hand reveals how you feel, how you behave instinctively, and what you are like in private. The lines in the palm of the passive hand highlight your capabilities and reflect your childhood and early years. You could say that this hand reflects the *inner* you.

Brain Power

Psychologists have carried out lots of research into left- and right-handedness and they have discovered that each of the two hemispheres of our brain controls different functions. On a right-handed person, the left side deals with reading, math, speech and logical processes.

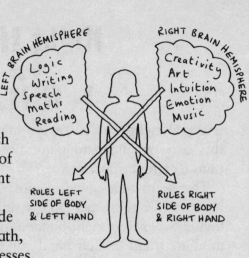

LEFT BRAIN HEMISPHERE
Logic
Writing
Speech
Maths
Reading

RIGHT BRAIN HEMISPHERE
Creativity
Art
Intuition
Emotion
Music

RULES LEFT SIDE OF BODY & LEFT HAND

RULES RIGHT SIDE OF BODY & RIGHT HAND

The right side controls the emotions, intuition, musical and artistic talents and all creative expression. For left-handed people, this is simply reversed.

The research has also revealed a strange cross-over effect, showing that the left side of the brain controls the right side of the body, and the right side of the brain controls the left side. This means that in a right-handed person the left side of the brain - which deals with the rational processes of reading and logic - is linked to the right hand, and information from that side of the brain is registered on this hand. The right side of the brain - which deals with the creative, emotional processes - is linked to the left hand, therefore that information is shown on this hand. Remember, this is completely reversed in people who are left-handed.

These links explain why each hand contains different information about us and why we have to read both hands to get a complete picture of a person.

About left-handed people

Only about thirteen per cent of people are left-handed. Interestingly, more men than women are born left-handed.

In the past, being left-handed was thought to be evil, so children who were born left-handed were forced to use their right hands. Quite cruel methods were used to achieve this, such as strapping down a child's left arm so that it couldn't be moved, or hitting the left hand with a stick whenever it was used.

Some famous left-handed people

Leonardo da Vinci
Charlie Chaplin
Horatio Nelson
Alexander the Great
Paul McCartney
Queen Victoria
Michelangelo
Julius Caesar
Judy Garland
Napoleon Bonaparte
Prince William
Bill Clinton

Are you ambidextrous?

A tiny percentage of people are truly ambidextrous, which means they can use both hands equally efficiently. However, even with truly ambidextrous people, there is often one hand that is slightly preferred over the other when it comes to writing or using tools, and it's this one that is considered the dominant hand.

Some people think the lines in our palms are made by the movements we make every day as we go about our business. They say that because we open and close our hands and move our fingers and thumbs thousands of times a day, the movements are bound to be responsible for forming those creases.

Now that's an interesting theory, but if you think about it logically you'll soon discover that it can't possibly be true.

For a start, babies are born with a fine set of lines already engraved into their palms. It's true, of course, that even unborn babies wiggle their fingers and open and clench their tiny fists while they're still in the womb, but you wouldn't expect their little movements to form that many lines in their hands in such a few months.

Also, since all unborn babies must do roughly the same things while they're developing, you'd expect, according to this theory, that all babies would be born with exactly the same lines - but they aren't.

And another thing. If the lines were formed by the movements of our hands, then you'd expect that people who do the same job - bricklayers, gardeners, cooks, computer operators, for example - would all develop similar lines. The fact that they don't proves that this theory is wrong.

The development of our lines
Like our fingerprints, our lines develop around the third

month of our development in the womb. And, also like our fingerprints and the shapes of our hands, we inherit our lines. If you compare your lines with those of the rest of your family, you may find, for example, that your head line might look like the one in your mother's hand, but your heart line might resemble your father's heart line. This would mean that you think like your mother, but you feel and react to situations in the same way as your father.

Don't forget, however, that although we all inherit our lines from our parents and our ancestors, you will never find another hand that will exactly match either of yours.

Changing lines

Although, when we're born, the major lines are already engraved in our hands, this doesn't mean that our lines remain the same for ever. If you take a hand print every year on your birthday, you'll see how the lines change as you mature and develop. For a start, they grow as your hand grows bigger, but they can shorten as well as lengthen, they can grow new branches and brand new sections, and they can split or break. They can also become thinner or thicker and, under certain rare circumstances, can even disappear altogether.

What can change our lines are the experiences we have. A major event will be reflected in our hands, but also simply changing our attitudes and opinions can sometimes produce remarkable changes in our lines. Our state of health is another big factor in what happens to our lines. For example, poor nutrition or a bad diet can affect the lines, making them appear thin, broken, and colorless.

The Major Lines

Take a look at this illustration showing the five most important lines in our hands.

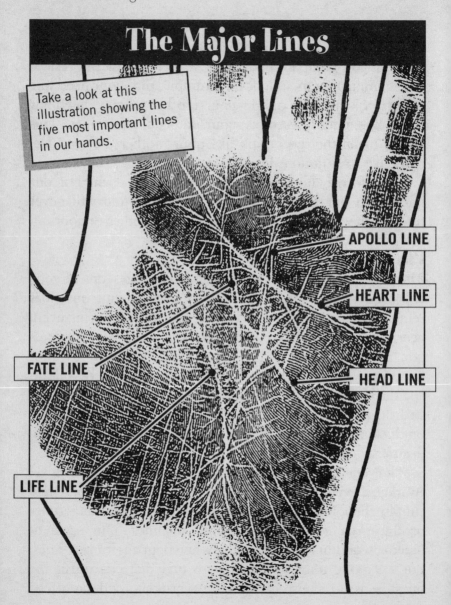

APOLLO LINE

HEART LINE

FATE LINE

HEAD LINE

LIFE LINE

Improving the diet and balancing the nutrition can dramatically heal the lines and bring back their true color.

So, as you can see, you're not necessarily stuck with any negative markings - they can and do change, and you are the one who has the power to change them. You could say that your fate is in your own hands.

Lots of lines vs few lines

When you start looking at people's hands, you'll notice that some palms are covered in a jumble of lines while others have so few that you would have a hard job to find even the five main lines in the palm.

In general, a very lined hand means that the person uses lots of nervous energy. Hands containing just a few lines go with a more placid temperament. If you know a real live wire, check out his or her hands. The chances are that those palms will be awash with lines!

Turning on the current

Think of the lines as cables carrying electrical energy along their length. To be serviceable, the cables need to be strong and in good condition. Any fraying or splitting will let the power seep out. Breaks in the cable can be dangerous and a heavy weight on top of it, such as the leg of a dresser, for example, could act as an obstruction, stopping the current getting through.

Our lines are like those electric cables. If we think of them as carrying energy, the condition of each line reveals the strength of the energy signal. If the line is weak, frayed-looking, or broken it tells us that the energy we possess isn't as strong as it could or should be. Or perhaps it can mean that our energies are being diverted into other areas, or temporarily blocked by circumstances beyond our control.

Each line represents a different type of energy. The head line, for instance, tells us how strong we are mentally, or how much "brain energy" we have. The life line tells us how strong we are physically, or what sort of vital "life force energy" we possess. The heart line reveals our "emotional energy." The fate line tells us about the energy we put into carrying out our duties and responsibilities. Finally, the Apollo line reveals our "creative energy."

Every one of us is different. Some people are strong and dominant. Some are dreamy and passive. Some love playing energetic games, while others prefer playing the piano. Whatever you are like, the lines in your hand will reflect your type of energy and your particular way of life. For example, people who are sporty and robust are likely to have thick, strong lines in their palms, but you'd expect to see much finer lines in the hands of people who are studious or sensitive.

Another thing to look out for when you're studying someone's hand is whether one line stands out more than the rest. Perhaps it's better constructed, stronger, thicker, deeper or brighter in color. Any line that stands out will reveal where that person's energies are concentrated. A stronger head line, for instance, suggests that the person prefers intellectual work, while a stronger life line would tell us that he or she puts more emphasis into physical work.

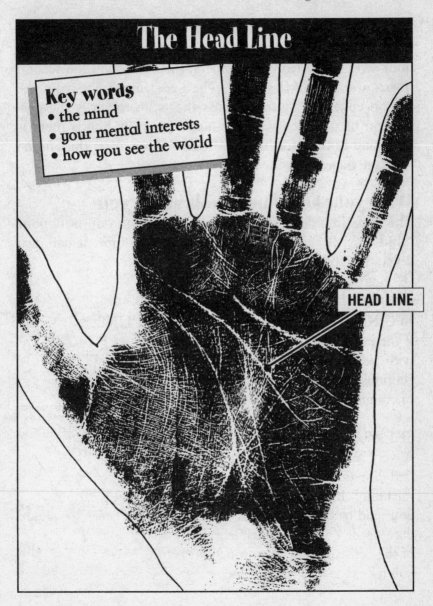

The Head Line

Key words
- the mind
- your mental interests
- how you see the world

HEAD LINE

Where to find the head line in your palm

The head line lies across the centre of the palm. Working your way down from the fingers, this is usually the second horizontal line in the palm. The head line starts from the thumb edge and sweeps across the palm towards the percussion or outer edge of the hand. In a few hands there is only one horizontal line, and this is known as the Simian line (see page 90).

What your head line reveals about you

The head line deals with the way you think and how your mind works. Depending on its length and type, it can also reveal the sort of subjects that interest you.

Different types of head lines

BEGINNING ATTACHED TO THE LIFE LINE

If the beginning of your head line merges with your life line, it means you're cautious and careful. This is the sign of common sense.

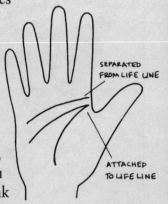

SEPARATED FROM LIFE LINE

ATTACHED TO LIFE LINE

SET APART FROM THE LIFE LINE

A very wide space between the head and life lines reveals an independent mentality. If you have this type of line, you tend to be impulsive and a bit of a dare-devil. You really must learn to think of the consequences of your actions before you take that leap in the dark.

STRAIGHT If your head line runs across the palm in a straight line, it means you're a logical sort of person with a sensible, realistic, and down-to-earth mentality. If your line is straight and short, ending beneath the middle finger, you're likely to enjoy practical subjects, sports, and working with your hands. If your line is straight but long, ending beneath the little finger, you're probably good at math and science.

CURVED A slightly curved line, ending on the palm beneath the ring or little fingers, is the sign of an investigative mentality and of someone who is good at all forms of communication. If your head line is like this, languages and literature are subjects you are likely to excel at. It means you have a creative turn of mind and you're especially good at dealing with people.

VERY STEEPLY CURVED A head line that is very steeply curved so that it sweeps a long way down, almost reaching the base of the palm, reveals a vivid imagination. If you have a line like this, you'll know how easily you can conjure up all sorts of fantasies in your own mind. If you're not careful, this sort of imagination can sometimes run away with itself and then you may become moody or melancholic, or start to dwell on negative thoughts. If, however, you learn to control your imaginative powers and use them creatively, you'll find that you have the ability to write wonderful stories or to paint fabulous pictures. With a head line like this, you could become famous one day!

The Simian Line

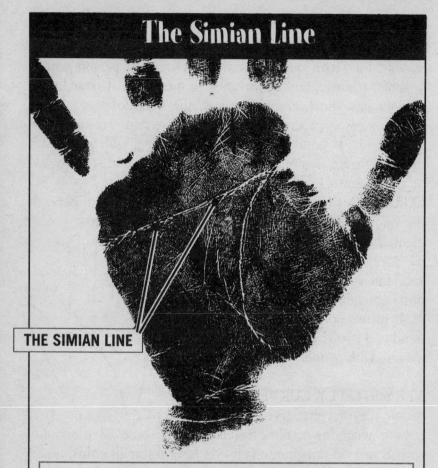

THE SIMIAN LINE

This is an unusual marking but it is found in some hands. It is formed when the head line merges with the heart line, so that instead of two creases there is only one across the top of the palm. If you have one of these, it shows you have tremendous powers of concentration. Also, you can be rather intense so you need to learn to relax and chill out.

The Life Line

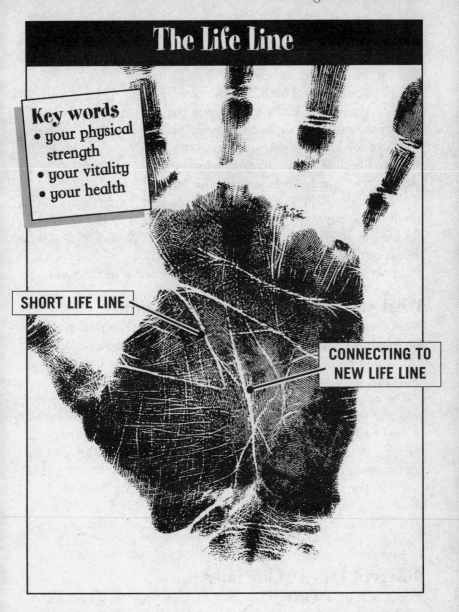

Key words
- your physical strength
- your vitality
- your health

SHORT LIFE LINE

CONNECTING TO NEW LIFE LINE

Where to find the life line in your palm

The life line is the semicircular crease that sweeps around the thumb. It starts on the edge of the palm, halfway between the base of the index finger and the crease at the base of the second section of the thumb. The line then curves downwards and in most hands curls around the base of the thumb, ending at the wrist. In some hands, however, you may find that either the life line itself, or a branch from the line, shoots out halfway down its course and ends at the wrist, towards the percussion or outer edge of the palm.

LIFE LINE SWINGING OUT TO CENTRE OF PALM

LIFE LINE AROUND THUMB

What your life line reveals about you

Some people have strange ideas about this line. They believe that the length of the life line reveals how long a person is going to live. If you ever hear anyone saying that a short life line means a short life, be sure to explain that this is absolute rubbish!

The length of the life line does not indicate how long an individual is going to live, because many a short line has been found in the hands of people who have lived well into their eighties and nineties, and long lines have been seen on those who have sadly passed away in their youth.

What your life line does reveal is the quality of your life. Depending on its type and how it's formed, this line will show how much energy you have, how strong and vital you are, and the state of your health.

Different types of life lines

A SHORT LIFE LINE If you have a short life line, examine it carefully and look further in towards the center of the palm for a

new section of life line that takes over from
the old one. Sometimes you may even find
a fine branch shooting out of the short
life line, linking it with the new one. If the
short life line is in your passive hand, it
could mean that either you or your parents
are no longer living in the country in which
you were born. If the marking is in your
dominant hand, it suggests that at some point
in your life you're going to make a major
change. Perhaps you will emigrate, perhaps you'll become mega
famous, perhaps you'll marry a pop star and join the jet set.
Whatever you end up doing, this big change will certainly broad-
en your horizons and take you to places you've never been to
before.

FORMING A WIDE ARC If your life
line forms a wide semicircle around
the thumb, it means you're a very
confident and out-going sort of person.
If your line also looks strong, it shows
that you enjoy good health and that, if
you do get ill, you have the power to
recover quickly.

FORMING A NARROW ARC If your life
line forms a tight semicircle around the thumb, it suggests that
you might lack self-confidence and this could make you shy and
timid. If you do have this line, look for a branch that shoots out
towards the center of your palm, as this will show that you will
develop your confidence and become a lot more adventurous
and out-going as you get older.

The Heart Line

Key words
- your emotions
- how you respond to other people
- your attitude to relationships

HEART LINE

Where to find the heart line in your palm

Working down from the fingers, the heart line is the first horizontal crease lying across the top of the palm. It begins at the percussion or outside edge of the palm and sweeps in to end some- where around the mount of Jupiter, beneath the index finger.

ENDING BETWEEN
1ST & 2ND FINGERS

ENDING AT BASE
OF INDEX FINGER

SHORT
HEART
LINE

ENDING ON
MOUNT OF
JUPITER

What your heart line reveals about you

Your heart line represents your emotions and innermost feelings. Depending on where in your hand it actually ends, this line will shed light on your attitudes to relationships - how you react to others and show affection to the people you love. This line can have several different endings. It's important to note exactly where and how it ends, as each position has a different meaning.

Different types of heart lines

ENDING ON THE JUPITER MOUNT If your heart line ends right in the center of the mount of Jupiter, underneath the index finger, it means you have a romantic nature. You tend to day- dream about relationships. You rather like the idea of fairy-tale romances - knights in shining armor or sleeping beauties - and you are a great believer in happy endings.

ENDING AT THE BASE OF THE INDEX FINGER This type of heart line reveals that you're a perfectionist. This means you hate making mistakes so much that you will work three, four, five times harder than anyone else to get things just right. You expect other people to be perfect, too, and when they're not, you get upset and feel let down. Perhaps at times like this you could remind yourself that people are only human and that mostly they do try to do their best. Love them for their good points, rather than picking out their faults. After all, if they love you, perhaps they could be shutting their own eyes to your shortcomings. Have you ever thought of that?

ENDING BETWEEN THE INDEX AND MIDDLE FINGERS If your heart line curves up to end on the web between your index and middle fingers, it means you have a realistic and mature attitude to relationships. You like to please the people you love by doing little things for them, but you may find it hard to actually tell them you love them. Perhaps you expect them to know how you feel and you think that words aren't necessary. However, it is important to express your feelings and if this is something your family finds difficult to do, one way around it is to write a little note and leave it under the pillow of the person you love. Alternatively, you could keep a private diary in which you describe all your feelings. You'd be surprised how much that can help to get things off your chest.

ENDING UNDER THE MIDDLE FINGER This line means you are a realist about relationships. But do try to put the people you love first, otherwise you could develop a tendency to be somewhat selfish.

ENDING IN A FORK This is the best possible type of ending for the heart line. It means you're sensitive and understanding and always prepared to see things from the point of view of the person you love.

The Fate Line

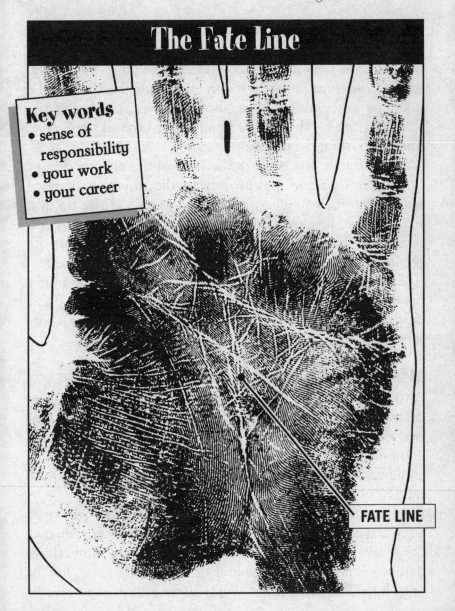

Key words
- sense of responsibility
- your work
- your career

FATE LINE

Where to find the fate line in your palm

Some people find it difficult to find their fate line because this line can start at various places in the palm. Generally, though, the fate line begins somewhere at the base of the palm near the wrist, then shoots upwards through the center of the hand. It should end on or around the Saturn mount, beneath the middle finger.

To find your line, start at the base of the palm and hunt for a line that travels upwards in the direction of your middle finger. It might start at your wrist and rise up in a straight line. It might begin on the mount of Luna, curving round and then slanting upwards. Or it could peel off the life line like a branch that shoots up to the middle finger.

If you can't find it at the base of your palm, yours might be one of those that starts a little higher up. But don't worry if you can't find it - some people don't have a fate line at all!

What your fate line reveals about you

Although it is called the *fate* line, it doesn't mean that your destiny is signed and sealed in this line. It's just a name that was given to it a long time ago when people thought differently about life and work. Remember that lines can and do change, and this one in particular is able to change quite readily as you go through life.

A strong, well-marked line means that you have plenty of common sense. You take your responsibilities seriously and tend not to let people down. This line also shows how ambitious and competitive you are. The clearer the line in your hand, the more effort you will put into your work and the better your chances of success will be.

This line also follows your progress through life and marks the events that take place. Breaks in this line simply register changes you make in your life or in your career. For example, moving to another part of the country, getting married, or changing your job will all be marked here either by a break in the line or by a new section that branches out from it.

Different types of fate lines

STARTING FROM THE CENTER AT THE BASE OF THE PALM This line means that, even from an early age, you know what you want to do in life and you work hard to achieve your goals. For example, you might have this type of line if you love animals and set your heart on becoming a vet. Or you might have a passion for aircraft and work really hard to become a pilot.

STARTING FROM THE MOUNT OF LUNA When your fate line begins here it shows that you like being with people and will probably choose a career which involves dealing with the public. Woking in a library, running a hotel, or presenting programs on television are some examples of jobs that require an ability to communicate well with people.

STARTING FROM THE LIFE LINE A fate line that starts from the life line, or from inside the life line, means that you have strong family commitments. This suggests that your career will somehow be linked with your parents or with other members of your family. Going into the family business is a good example of the meaning of this line.

STARTING HIGHER UP If the line is missing at the base of your hand but starts higher up, it means that you may not feel that things "click into place" for you until your late teens or early twenties. That's probably the time when you find your true vocation or suddenly realize what it is you want to do in life.

SO YOU DON'T HAVE A FATE LINE? If you don't have a fate line, or if yours is very faint at this stage in your life, it's quite possible that one will appear later on, or that your faint line will strengthen and thicken sometime in the future. Meanwhile, no fate line at all could mean you're an "easy come, easy go" sort of person, or that you can't decide right now what you want to do when you leave school. Your line will probably develop as your future becomes clearer to you, or later on when you decide on the career you want to follow.

WILL YOU BE FAMOUS? In most hands the fate line ends underneath the middle finger. In a few hands, however, this line travels towards the Saturn mount but suddenly changes direction and shoots off to end under the index finger. If your line does this, start practising your autograph now, because this is a sign that you could become a mega-star one day.

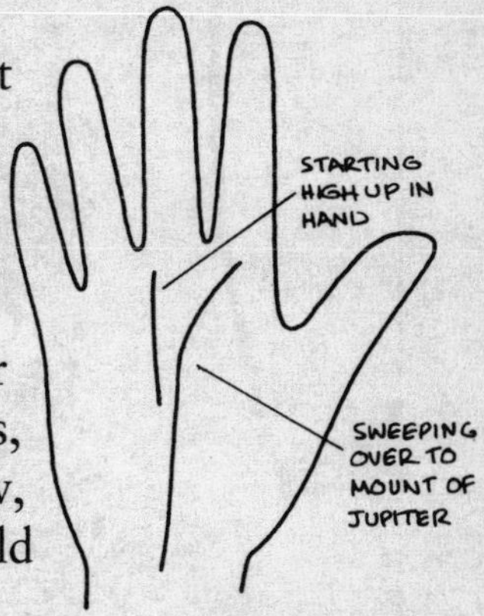

STARTING
HIGH UP IN
HAND

SWEEPING
OVER TO
MOUNT OF
JUPITER

The Apollo Line

Key words
- creativity
- happiness
- fame

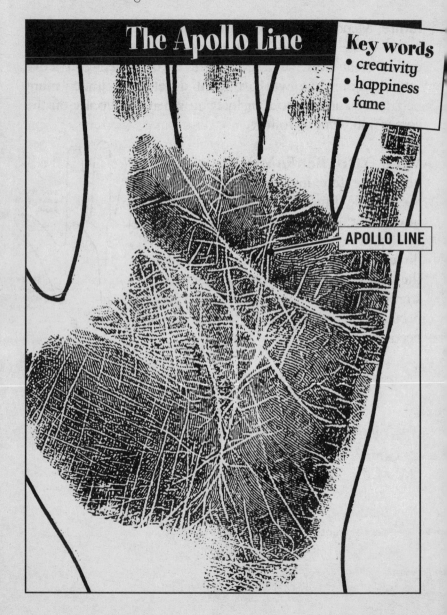

APOLLO LINE

Where to find the Apollo line in your palm

Like the fate line, the Apollo line can be hard to find and some hands may not have it at all. This is a vertical line but it hardly ever starts right at the base of the palm. In many hands it begins somewhere in the center of the palm, nearer the head line. Sometimes, it springs out of the fate line and looks like a branch that shoots up towards the ring finger. But in most hands it doesn't even start until after the heart line, where it runs up the Apollo mount. Wherever it begins, it always ends beneath the Apollo finger, which gives it its name.

What your Apollo line reveals about you

This line is also known as the Sun line. One reason for this is that people who have long, strong, clearly marked Apollo lines also have a sunny nature. If you have this line, it means you're a happy sort of person. You're probably very creative and using your artistic skills gives you enormous pleasure. In fact, the stronger and longer this line, the more successful and contented you will be in life.

Different types of Apollo lines

BEGINNING AT THE BASE OF THE PALM It's extremely rare for this line to start right down at the base of the palm. If you have one like this, you're not only an exception, you're also a budding genius! Child actors, gifted young musicians and teenage pop stars are the sort of people who might have a line like this.

STARTING HIGHER UP IN PALM NEAR HEAD LINE

STARTING FROM BASE

BEGINNING NEAR TO THE HEAD LINE You may have to wait until your thirties or forties before your talents are recognized. If you keep putting in the effort, however, you will be successful sooner or later.

STARTING
ABOVE
HEART LINE

STARTING
FROM
BRANCH
OFF FATE
LINE

BEGINNING FROM THE FATE LINE With this line in your hand, you're bound to make a success of your creative talents through your own hard work.

BEGINNING ABOVE THE HEART LINE An Apollo line that begins above the heart line promises a happy life when you're older. That may seem a long way off, but it's comforting to know that you will be loved and still able to enjoy life when you retire. If you have this type of Apollo line, tuck that thought away in the back of your mind and remind yourself now and again throughout your life - particularly when you're feeling low - that good times lie ahead.

DO YOU HAVE MORE THAN ONE APOLLO LINE? Two or three parallel Apollo lines running up your hand show you have lots of different talents. Three lines, especially above the heart line, are a sign of good fortune and mean that you're lucky with money.

The Minor Lines

So far, only the five major lines have been described, but you may have noticed by now that a lot of palms also contain a good many more lines. The others are known as the minor lines, and they can give us even more information to add to our personality profiles.

See if you can find any of these in your own hands.

The Mercury line

WHERE TO FIND IT If you have it, this line slants across your palm from the life line up to the mount of Mercury and ends under the little finger.

WHAT IT MEANS This line is also known as the health line, so you might be quite happy not to have one at all! If it is visible and it looks broken or twisted, it may suggest that you need to take care of your health because you could be more prone to illness than other people. This line is also a reminder that you should get plenty of rest, exercise, and fresh air, and you will need to have a well-balanced diet throughout your life. If you have two of these creases, the second one is a business line. It shows that you have good business skills and a terrific ability to make money!

The Bow of Intuition

WHERE TO FIND IT This is a rare marking that is seen on only a few hands. If you have it, you'll find it towards the outer edge of your palm. It is a semicircular line which starts from the mount of Luna, curls up and around to end on the mount of Mercury.

GIRDLE OF VENUS

MERCURY LINE

BOW OF INTUITION

WHAT IT MEANS This marking is seen in the hands of very intuitive people. If you have it in your palm, you may have noticed that at times you get really strong hunches about people and events. Certainly, this line says you should trust your instincts because you may have what's known as second sight (an ability to predict what's going to happen in the future). Also, learn to listen to your dreams - they're probably vivid but they could also be prophetic.

listen to your dreams

The Girdle of Venus

WHERE TO FIND IT This is a semicircular line found on the palm above the heart line. It forms a sort of necklace looped beneath the ring and middle fingers. It's not usual to find it as a complete line and more often than not it's made up of broken little sections. However, don't worry if you don't have one - it's really quite a rare marking, and you're probably better off without it, anyway.

WHAT IT MEANS If you possess this line it shows you're a sensitive person. You tend to feel easily put down and take slights personally, even when insults or negative comments are not aimed at you. What you really need to do is to find a way to boost your self-confidence. Find out what you're good at and develop those talents so that you can be proud of your achievements. One talent this line reveals is acting ability. Even when you tell a story you have the knack of bringing it alive. So think about joining an amateur dramatics group - it just might lead to an amazingly successful career. But, above all, do learn to laugh at yourself.

Other Markings To Look Out For

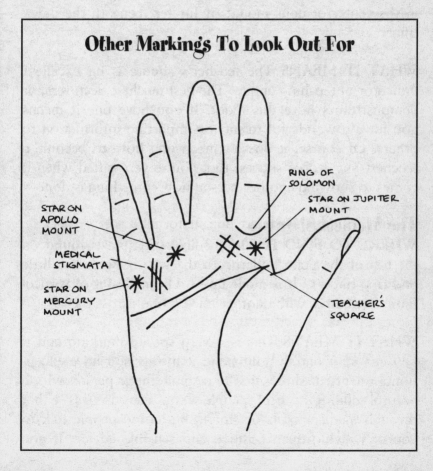

RING OF SOLOMON

STAR ON JUPITER MOUNT

STAR ON APOLLO MOUNT

MEDICAL STIGMATA

STAR ON MERCURY MOUNT

TEACHER'S SQUARE

If you look hard enough, you'll find lots of other little markings that have some very interesting meanings. See if you can find any of the following in your hand.

The Teacher's Square
WHERE TO FIND IT This marking is made up of four little lines formed into a square. If you have one, you'll find it in the center of your mount of Jupiter, beneath the index finger.

WHAT IT MEANS The teacher's square is an excellent indicator of teaching ability. The best teachers, lecturers, or demonstrators have this mark. If you have one it means you have a wonderful talent for imparting information to others. Of course, it doesn't mean you have to become a teacher, but it does suggest that you're very gifted when it comes to showing another person how something is done.

The Medical Stigmata
WHERE TO FIND IT The medical stigmata is found on the top of the palm underneath the web between the little and ring fingers. It is made up of a little cluster of vertical lines, sometimes with another line cutting across them.

WHAT IT MEANS This is a very special marking and if you can spot one in your hand it means you have exceptional talents. It shows you're a sympathetic person with a natural ability to heal people. You can do this either through medical skills or simply by letting people talk to you and giving them positive and sensible advice. If you have this marking, you should think about a career in medicine. You could train to become a doctor, a nurse, or a vet. If you don't like the sight of blood, there are lots of other ways you can help to heal people. You could become a psychologist, a counsellor, or an optician, for example. Or else you could think about aromatherapy, acupuncture, herbalism, and other sorts of alternative healing therapies.

The Ring of Solomon

WHERE TO FIND IT This marking is a semicircular ring on the mount of Jupiter encircling the base of the index finger.

WHAT IT MEANS The ring of Solomon is a sign of wisdom. If you have this marking, you were born with what's known as an old head on young shoulders, which means that you are very mature for your age.

Thank Your Lucky Stars

There is one marking that, if found on any of three particular places in your palm, almost certainly guarantees that you will find success in life. This marking is the star.

The star is made up of several little lines that cross over each other like an asterisk. It must stand completely alone on one of the following mounts:

ON THE MOUNT OF MERCURY A clearly formed star here shows you have the ability to become successful in business. With this star in your hand, you could make a lot of money one day.

ON THE MOUNT OF APOLLO With a star on this mount, you will have opportunities to find success with your creative talents. This mark is a sign that you could become wealthy and even famous.

ON THE MOUNT OF JUPITER This is perhaps the very best place in the hand to find a star, because here it tells of an outstandingly happy and fortunate life.

5 TALKING HANDS

The gestures we make with our hands can reveal our hidden thoughts and feelings. So, if you're going to analyze people's hands, you must also take note of how they use their hands when they are talking to you or to other people.

You'll be amazed at the secrets you can discover about others simply by observing their hand gestures!

Limp hands vs rapid movements

How we move our hands is one of the telltale signs of how we're feeling, both physically and mentally. For example, a doctor can immediately tell a lot about your health by the way you hold your hands when you walk into the surgery. If your hands are limp and listless, you obviously don't have very much energy. You are either feeling unwell, or you're sad and depressed.

Alternatively, if your hand movements are rapid, possibly even jerky, you are nervous or anxious about something. You may be hyperactive or have just had a fright, or perhaps you are afraid of something. Whatever the reason, fidgety movements often mean that you need to calm down.

If you want to come across as confident and poised, try to control your hand gestures. Make your movements natural and fluid. Keep them flowing in an easy and graceful manner. Practice doing this. You'll find that if you can control your gestures, you'll feel much more in control of yourself and of the situation.

Outward gestures vs inward gestures

Some people fling their arms out a lot when they're talking to you. They spread out their hands and reveal their palms. This sort of person is very outgoing, extroverted, and expressive. Open hands with palms up are signs of friendliness and honesty. People who use their hands like this are saying they have nothing to hide and that you can trust them. They're also saying that they're interested in you and in what's going on in the outside world.

People whose hand and arm movements tend to point towards their own bodies are more introverted types. They may be shy or timid, or they may be egocentric, meaning that they always put themselves first. When the gestures point inwards it is a sign of someone who is guarded and defensive. And beware of people who keep their hands firmly stuffed into their pockets while they're speaking to you - unless, of course, you're in the middle of a snow storm! In normal circumstances this could be a sign of a very secretive nature. You may need to ask yourself, what has this person got to hide?

Acting the part

Our gestures are said to be a form of silent communication. If you're uneasy about someone, or unsure whether he or she is telling you the truth, forget what's being said and watch the gestures instead, because these don't lie. Someone who is sincere, for example, will have easy-flowing hand movements and open palms. Someone who isn't being honest may have fidgety movements or clenched fists that hide the palm. Actors have to learn all about gestures. The best ones get all the gestures right. The bad ones don't, so we don't believe in the characters they are playing.

What's in a Handshake?

A handshake is a form of greeting that reveals an enormous amount about a person, so it's especially interesting when you're meeting someone new. Next time you're introduced to a person, see what clues you can pick up from the handshake alone.

A weak handshake

If, when you shake hands with someone, the hand is limp and barely grips your own, it means that person isn't very assertive and perhaps lacks confidence. If the hand is also sweaty, he or she may be anxious about the situation. If that happens, perhaps you could smile or say something reassuring that will put the person at ease.

A forceful handshake

There is something wrong with a handshake that's too strong. You know the sort of thing - your hand is caught in a vice-like grip which can actually be quite painful. A person who shakes hands with you like that is trying to show you who's the boss! This person is rather aggressive and wants to unnerve you.

If this happens, look the person straight in the eye and take a tiny step forward as you say "How do you do?" This will subtly tell the person that you won't allow yourself to be intimidated. By taking that tiny step forward, you're doing two things. First, you're stepping into that person's space, as if to say you're accepting the challenge. And secondly, with luck it will force him or her to take a step back. If that happens it means the person has recognized that you are not someone who is willing to be bossed around.

A confident handshake

When you meet someone for the first time, make sure your hand is dry before you offer it in greeting (you can discreetly blot it against the side of your thigh before extending your hand). Then, when you take the other person's hand, apply just enough pressure so that your grip is firm but not over-strong. Hold the other person's hand for a few seconds, gently shaking it – but don't pump it forcefully up and down! Smile charmingly - and in this brief moment you will have given the impression of being confident, open, and friendly.

How long should a handshake last?

This depends both on the circumstances and on who is involved in the greeting. When two people meet for the first time, the hands should be clasped for just a few seconds. There's a hint of cunning or deceit in a stranger who holds your hand for too long. This person is not quite sincere. But someone who holds your hand too briefly is obviously not interested in you, or is impatient to get away.

Handshakes can sometimes carry subtle messages of sexual attraction, however. For example, if a man holds a woman's hand for a little longer than normal, or applies just a tiny bit more pressure than is usual, he's silently telling her that he finds her extremely attractive!

Some Fascinating Facts

1

The earliest-known hand prints were stamped on the walls of Stone Age caves and have been discovered in countries as far apart as Spain and Australia. This means that men and women have been interested in their hands since Neolithic times.

That's interesting

Uugh!

2

People have been reading hands for thousands of years. The earliest records, from China, date back to about 3000 BC. That's five thousand years ago! There are also some ancient Indian books still in existence which date back four thousand years and give clear instructions on how to read hands.

3

When the printing press was invented in the fifteenth century, one of the first books to be printed was on hand reading! It was written by Johann Hartlieb, a Viennese monk.

4 In the first century AD, Galen, the father of medicine, said that a doctor wasn't fit to give advice to patients if he didn't know how to read a hand properly. Later, in the Middle Ages, hand reading was taught at the universities. Doctors learned all about the markings in the hand as part of their medical training. The markings helped them to diagnose their patients' illnesses.

5

Lots of medical research has been carried out on hand markings throughout the twentieth century and the findings have been fascinating. The researchers have discovered a link between our health and our skin markings. For example, people with certain genetic disorders, such as Down's syndrome, have specific patterns in their hands which are only found in this group of people. In the last few years, researchers have found another important link. They have proved that people who are prone to heart disease, or high blood pressure, have a particular type of fingerprint pattern on their fingertips.

6 The technical name for the study of skin patterns is "dermatoglyphics." These patterns are found on the palms and fingers of our hands and on the soles of our feet. The patterns are made up of ridges and grooves because the skin in these areas has to be tougher and more resilient than anywhere else in the body.

7 Our fingerprints are made by the tiny little beads of sweat and oil that come out from minute pores that lie alongside the ridges making up the patterns of the skin. No matter how much you scrub yourself, or how clean your hands are, you will still leave your prints on whatever you touch. A fingerprint that is left at the scene of a crime is known as a latent.

8 When, in 1948, a little girl was murdered in a town in the North of England, the police were determined to catch the murderer. They took the fingerprints of every single man in and around the town and matched each one to a latent they had found at the scene of the crime. The police fingerprinted 47,000 men before they found their match and were able to convict the person who had carried out that terrible crime.

9

The bodies of Egyptian mummies have been so well preserved that much of their skin still remains intact. Recently, when scientists were examining one of these ancient mummies, they were amazed to find that they could still see the prints clearly on the mummy's fingertips even after all these years!

10

Human beings are not the only animals to have patterns on their fingers and palms. Monkeys and apes have similar types of patterns on their hands and feet. Gorillas have them on their knuckles, too. This is because they lean on the back of their hands as they walk along, so that part of their hand is like a second palm. Other monkeys, such as the Woolley Monkey, have fingerprint-patterned skin on their tails! This is because their tails are like extra hands which they use to grab onto branches when they swing from tree to tree.

11

Patterns similar to our fingerprints can be found elsewhere in the animal kingdom, in some surprising places. For instance, did you know that the pattern on the skin covering a cow's muzzle is unique? And so is the pattern on your dog's nose. If you take a print of your puppy's muzzle, you'll be able to use it to identify him should he ever be dognapped!

12

Our brains are divided into areas, each one controlling a different part of the body. These areas are not all the same size. Some are tiny while others are large - it all depends on whether the body part that is being controlled needs a lot of brain power or not. The area devoted to the hand is HUGE. It's one of the largest areas of the brain. This means that the hand needs masses of brain space because it is so complex and so important!

13

The hand contains 27 bones. There are twelve in the fingers and two in the thumb. Five bones are arranged in a fan shape across the palm, and eight bones make up the wrist. These bones are attached to 37 muscles which enable us to move our hands and control our fingers with exquisitely minute precision.

14

Anne Boleyn, the second wife of King Henry VIII, is said to have had six fingers on each hand. Her portraits show her with long sleeves because, it is believed, she was always trying to hide her hands. In those days, if you had an extra finger on your hand, people thought you were a witch.

15

The man with the longest fingernails in the world is an Indian called Shridhar Chillal. In 1996 the nail on his left thumb measured 135 centimeters, but the one on his little finger was only 117 centimeters long! He hasn't cut his nails since 1952, when he was fifteen years old.

122 • Hand Reading

Index

Put your hand print here ...

... and here!